SUCCESS
WITHOUT
SUCCESS

SUCCESS
WITHOUT
SUCCESS

GEORGE BURGESS

Whitaker House

SUCCESS WITHOUT SUCCESS

ISBN: 0-88368-369-5
Printed in the United States of America
Copyright © 1995 by Whitaker House

Whitaker House
580 Pittsburgh Street
Springdale, PA 15144

1 2 3 4 5 6 7 8 9 10 11 / 05 04 03 02 01 00 99 98 97 96 95

DEDICATION

I dedicate this book to the risen Christ for He freely offered up His life to save a sinner like me. As undeserving as I am, He has likewise allowed me to write this book to His glory, thereby proving once again, our Lord is a God of grace and mercy! May Jesus Christ be praised!

ACKNOWLEDGMENTS

I would like to express my thanks to Carol A. and Elizabeth B. Pingree who sacrificed their time to make important contributions to this book. I would like to thank all my family and friends for their love and support throughout the years!

Special thanks go to my wife Carol, my children Joel, Jamie, Joshua, Julianne, and Joy Marie; my mother Janet; sisters Barbara, Sharon, and Liz; my grandparents the Oldham's; and my aunt Pat. My profound gratitude is extended to my parents-in-law Al and Edith Abrahamsen. Each of you have played a very special role in my life, and in one way or another contributed to the making of this book. I love you and thank each of you!

CONTENTS

1

PERSPECTIVES OF SUCCESS

FRAME ME MORE AND MORE INTO THE LIKENESS OF THY SON, JESUS CHRIST, THAT LIVING IN THY FEAR, AND DYING IN THY FAVOR; I MAY IN THY APPOINTED TIME ATTAIN THE RESURRECTION OF THE JUST UNTO ETERNAL LIFE...UNITE US ALL IN PRAISING AND GLORIFYING THEE IN ALL OUR WORKS.[1]

GEORGE WASHINGTON
FIRST PRESIDENT OF THE UNITED STATES
—FROM HIS PRAYER JOURNAL

In the summer of 1956, movie starlet Marilyn Monroe was on top of the world. She had just married playwright Arthur Miller and was entering her most successful years as an actress. Because of her enormous popularity she was well on her way to becoming a film legend. Tragically, in the summer of 1962, her success ended when she was found dead in her Brentwood, California, home. The coroner's report stated that she had died of a barbiturates overdose.

In the winter of 1942, award winning inventor Edwin H. Armstrong had reached the pinnacle of his career. He held patents on the three basic electronic circuits central to modern radio, radar, and television. He had already been awarded the highest honor in U.S. science, the Franklin Medal, and was considered by many to rank with such electrical greats as Alexander Graham Bell and Guglielmo Marconi. Sadly, during the winter of 1954, Armstrong took his life by jumping from his apartment window in New York's River House section.

In the spring of 1941, internationally renowned banker Leon Fraser had emerged as the key spokesman for the banking community of the world. He was revered as an essential element in advancing the cause of an international monetary cooperation. Woefully, in the spring of 1945, he returned to his boyhood home of North Granville, New York, to take his life.

These are only a small sample of the many men and women who have reached the heights of worldly success, only to abandon it. The cup of success was sweet and refreshing at first, but they soon realized its emptiness and despair. These three individuals are a microcosm of mankind's lifelong struggle to succeed. We see man vigorously pursuing a form of success which lacks the substance of true success. He foolishly spends his time, energy, and resources to obtain a success that is here one moment and gone the next.

At every turn we see the multitudes making their way toward the humanistic summit of success, hoping they will partake of the true fruits of victory. When analyzing the shallowness of man's earthly endeavors, we can't help but feel a sense of sorrow for the many who have willfully chosen to waste their lives investing in a success, without true success.

Perhaps you have never listened to the quiet pleas of those such as Marilyn, Ed, and Leon, people whose examples sorrowfully cry out a warning to us all. They gave everything to obtain a man-centered success, only to find their reward being a handful of emptiness.

As we seek to better understand the true meaning of success, let us learn from the tragic examples of Marilyn, Ed, and Leon. Let us together wrestle with the concept which guides and motivates every aspect of our lives. As we explore this most important subject, let us allow the Holy Spirit to cleanse and conform us into the very image of true success.

The word *success* is one of the most exhilarating terms in our language. Just the mention of it tends to produce joyous thoughts of self-gratification. The concept is easily grasped on the surface, yet when closely examined it is very complex. In formulating our personal views of success, we draw from our past experiences, attitudes, emotions, and the body of knowledge we have accumulated since birth. Our understanding is also influenced by vocation, religion, and even nationality.

The various factors that go into the development of one's view naturally produce diversity among men. This diversity is compounded by man's limited ability to discern between genuine and counterfeit forms of success. Such confusion causes most people to spend their lives pursuing a form of success which fails to transcend the feelings and values of mere men.

MAN-CENTERED

We may consider the meaning and purpose of success from one of two perspectives. The first and most common is the man-centered or humanistic view. Its main objective is self-exultation. More specifically, it centers on the fulfillment of some form of mental, emotional, material, or religious accomplishment.

Because of its subjectivity, the criterion for success tends to vary from person to person. In the absence of universal absolutes, one man's success may be another man's failure.

Scripture clearly tells us the man-centered approach is doomed to eternal failure. This becomes evident when we consider the message of the Preacher in Ecclesiastes 1:2-3 (NAS): *"'Vanity of vanities! All is vanity.' What advantage does man have in all his work, which he does under the sun?"* In a forthright manner, the Preacher declares that there is nothing man can do in the flesh which transcends the realm of vanity. He further illustrates his point by directing our attention to the single area where most spend the vast majority of their time—the work arena—where many find a sense of worth and even personal satisfaction. Through it some have built solid reputations or amassed large sums of money. In one brief statement, the Preacher proclaims to mankind that all labor is vanity.

Throughout his proclamation, the Preacher informs us that regardless of our expert craftsmanship, credible reputation, or the amount of money gained, all labor for the purpose of self-exultation is vanity. As if to discourage us from seeking out any other means of self-gratification, the Preacher goes on to

13

proclaim in Ecclesiastes 1:4-2:23 that all human wisdom, pleasure, wealth, and possessions are futile.

Such things are *"striving after the wind,"* a wind which may be neither caught nor contained and has no eternal value or success. In his great wisdom the Preacher understood the folly of pursuing a wind-like success. He knew that such success could never be grasped and that true success means much more than mere worldly accomplishments.

GOD-CENTERED

As gloomy as things may seem, the Preacher does not leave us without hope or direction. Thankfully, he directs us toward the Provider of true success, hoping to refocus our perception by adjusting our vision of reality. He does so through skillfully drawing our attention away from a gloomy, earthly perspective to an exalted, godly one.

In verse 25 the Preacher asks *"For who can eat and who can have enjoyment without Him* [God]?" The obvious response is "no one!" He then points out that good things come to those who are *"good in His sight"* (v. 26). Those who are good in His sight are God's spiritual children. His children are different

14

because they see human wisdom, pleasure, wealth, and possessions from a godly perspective. They understand that from cover to cover, the Bible demonstrates true prosperity and success as a result of the Father's hand.

Success in Scripture is seen in terms of the glorification of God through the acknowledgment and application of His will in our lives. A wealth of worship, obedience, faith, hope, and love, formulates the core of all true success. Biblical success cannot be achieved apart from the Lord but rather through Him.

Unlike the uncertainty of humanism, Christianity maintains absolute standards that distinguish between success and failure. These standards are clearly revealed through the divinely inspired Word of God. Because the glorification of God is objective in nature, the achievement of it is concrete and measurable. From God's perspective, a material gain or loss does not dictate the degree of one's success. The heart and soul of true success revolves around pleasing God regardless of the circumstances.

The Lord's view of success is encapsulated in Deuteronomy 6:5: *"Love the LORD your God with all your heart and with all your soul and with all your strength."* The greatest commandment informs us that true success

15

springs forth from the depths of our inner-most being and freely offers up all we have for the purpose of glorifying God. The glorification of God must be at the very heart of all our endeavors, no matter how big or small. (See Matt. 5:16 and 1 Cor. 10:31) If our purpose is anything less than the absolute glorification of God, then our labor is in vain.

Christ addresses the sin of self-righteousness in the parable of the Pharisee and the tax collector. He does so to expose the conceit of those who affirm a man-centered success. In the parable Jesus told of two men who went to the temple to pray; one a Pharisee and the other a tax collector.

> *The Pharisee stood up and prayed about himself: "God, I thank you that I am not like all other men—robbers, evildoers, adulterers—or even like this tax collector. I fast twice a week and give a tenth of all I get." But the tax collector stood at a distance. He would not even look up to heaven, but beat his breast and said, "God, have mercy on me, a sinner." I tell you that this man, rather than the other, went home justified before God. For everyone who exalts himself will be humbled, and he who humbles himself will be exalted.* (Luke 18:11-14)

As seen in the parable, Christ contrasts between counterfeit and genuine forms of success. In the case of the Pharisee, highly regarded as a religious man, Jesus revealed the man's object of affirmation to be himself. The Pharisee self-righteously stood before God, informing Him of his great worth. Christ notes that the self-exaltation of the Pharisee was misguided (v. 14), in choosing to affirm himself rather than God.

We also see Christ using the example of a much despised tax collector (v. 13) to establish His concept of true success. As sinful as the tax collector was, he fully understood his depravity, and humbly he rightly chose to cry out to God for mercy. In doing so, his failure enabled true success, because the object of his affirmation was neither himself, nor his wealth, but rather the Creator.

Clearly the parable teaches that the highly religious Pharisee labored in vain, while the sinful tax collector tasted success. The Pharisee failed as he willfully chose a counterfeit, while the sinner succeeded by pursuing that which was genuine.

The prayer of the misguided Pharisee reminds me of a quote I once heard from a poem called "Song of Myself" by Walt Whitman. Whitman begins the poem by saying "I celebrate myself and sing myself, And what I assume you shall assume."[2] At the very heart of this poem lies a pompous attitude which seeks to proclaim self above all else. Such feelings become evident when the poet later declares, "And nothing, not God, is greater to one than one's self is."[3] Whitman exalts a philosophy which maintains little room for the God of the Bible, a philosophy that celebrates man and the conceit which motivates him to such high levels of self-adulation.

The Pharisee in similar fashion stands before God singing the praise of self. Like Whitman, he wrongly assumes his accuracy. Tragically, the Pharisee foolishly believes that what he assumes is also God's position. Sadly, he and many others have blindly trusted in a godless self-assurance.

As we continue on in our study of true success, let us determine to no longer be satisfied with a false assurance. Let us no longer attempt to satisfy a righteous God with the foolishness of a man-centered success. Let us not forget the similarity between the Pharisee's religiosity and Whitman's blatant humanism. Neither approach procures favor in God's eyes. Therefore, let us fix our eyes upon the Author and Finisher of true success in order to claim His presence in our lives.

2

SUCCESS IN THE BEGINNING

I LONG TO ACCOMPLISH A GREAT AND NOBLE
TASK, BUT IT IS MY CHIEF DUTY TO ACCOMPLISH
TASKS AS THOUGH THEY WERE GREAT AND
NOBLE.[4]

> HELEN KELLER
> AUTHOR AND LECTURER
> DEAF AND BLIND

If thinking in terms of gathering historical facts and figures, clearly the Bible is not a modern-day history book. Yet as we seek to better understand the history recorded in it, we may be assured that the records and recollections are accurate. They are accurate because God Himself is the Author of Scripture. Thus, we may be assured that the accounts described are neither myths nor fairy tales but rather the literal unfolding of mankind's history of success and failure. It is essential to recognize that from the very beginning, God provided man with everything necessary for his success.

19

A PURE AND SINLESS NATURE

In the beginning, God created man with a pure and sinless nature. Genesis 1:27 says, "*So God created man in his own image, in the image of God he created him; male and female He created them.*" Here it states that "*God created man in his own image.*" It also implies that man was created with a moral likeness similar to God's. We know from other passages that God is perfect and sinless (Psa. 5:4; Hab. 1:13; James 1:13). To the degree that man was created in God's image, he too was created perfect and sinless.

A PERFECT ENVIRONMENT

We see the commencement of God's plan in Genesis 1:1: "*In the beginning God created the heavens and the earth.*" It is important to note that "*in the beginning*" God was present. To assume otherwise would be to deny the existence of God and the validity of His Word. We also see that God was actively involved in the work of creation. Things did not just happen their way into existence; God created a perfect place for man to abide. Indeed, we may confidently declare if God were not both present and actively involved, there would have been no Creation at all!

As we skim through the first chapter of Genesis, we realize that God not only created the heavens and the earth but many other things as well. He created the oceans, light, land, vegetation, and all living creatures. Upon completion of His creative work, God surveyed all He had accomplished and perceived that *"it was very good"* (v. 31). This confirms that God saw His entire creation as perfect and lacking nothing. This is important because it helps us understand the original nature of the world God created.

By carefully examining the composition of *"the heavens and the earth,"* it becomes apparent that God created them in such a way as to perfectly suit all of man's needs. We know that in order to survive, man needs air to breathe, water to drink, and food to nourish his body. God created a habitat which consistently and harmoniously works together to provide man's essentials. This leads us to believe that it was God's intention from the very beginning to prepare a perfect environment, capable of affording man every opportunity to be content, cared for, and successful in God's eyes.

When God situated Adam and Eve in the garden, it was no coincidence they were made to live there by themselves. In fact, we may assume this was a deliberate act on God's part.

The God who created all things including man, maintained the ability to create many others if he so desired. The fact that God created only one couple is not a testimony of His inability but rather an affirmation of His divine will. God, in His perfect wisdom, designed for Adam and Eve to initially dwell in the garden by themselves. In Genesis 2:15 God began this trend by creating man and placing him in the garden by himself for a short duration. Soon after Eve was created joining Adam in their exclusive garden paradise.

God likewise saw fit to limit man's activities to a handful of chores. God made it clear that man was to care for himself, (Gen. 2:16-17) to tend the garden, (Gen. 2:15) and name the animals (Gen. 2:20). Because of God's general oversight, we may presume that none of these tasks were overly taxing to man.

Why did God choose to isolate man from others and limit his activities? It appears in the early days of man's existence, God sought to curb the number of distractions dividing man's time and energy. By nature man is easily distracted, and Adam was no exception. For Adam and Eve to have every possible opportunity to learn those things necessary to succeed, God allowed His creature to reside in a perfect environment, one which was regulated in such a way as to encourage man to focus on God and their assigned duties.

It appears God had two specific reasons for doing this, the first being a desire to fellowship with man. Had God created other humans it is likely man's attention would have been divided, (1 Cor. 7:32-35) and the opportunity for true fellowship diminished. Secondly, Adam and Eve most likely needed time to acclimate themselves to their new surroundings. Thus, the best way to provide for these needs would have been through a period of isolation and limitation.

When God created man, He did not create a robot with a computerized memory that need only be fed factual information. God created a man in His own image, who was capable of reasoning, communicating thoughts and emotions, and endowed with a desire to maintain personal relationships. The man God created was very complex and needed time to adjust to his new surroundings and relationships.

During this time of adjustment, it appears God was Adam and Eve's only source of knowledge and understanding. This is not to say that man did not learn through observation but rather God was their only teacher. Initially, there were no other influences distracting them from those things which God wanted them to learn. Because of their isolation, man and his wife were able to focus solely upon God and the things God felt were most important. Ultimately, God wanted to afford them with every opportunity to learn those things necessary to succeed in God's world.

Throughout Scripture, we see numerous examples of the Lord being a God of order (1 Cor. 14:33). We see in the first and second chapters of Genesis that God made His goals for man very clear; there was no discrepancy or room for confusion. For instance, God intended man to care for himself. We see God instructing man to do so when He states, *"You are free to eat from any tree in the garden* (Gen. 2:16). We see God providing the food, directing man to it, and informing him of its purpose. Clearly, God set specific goals for man. Goals that were understandable and attainable.

God continues this pattern of instruction by reinforcing the positive command with a negative counterpart, *"but you must not eat from the tree of the knowledge of good and evil"* (v. 17). God did not want to see His noblest creature stumble, thus, in a simple yet forceful manner, God again sought to develop man's understanding through contrasting the difference between acceptable and unacceptable behavior. God graciously concludes His lesson by explaining to man the consequences of ignoring His directive, *"for when you eat of it* (the tree) *you will surely die"* (v. 17). In order to make certain that man fully understood the magnitude of his potential disobedience, God makes His feelings known. If man failed to acknowledge his teacher's instruction, he had no one to blame but himself.

Ultimately, the main point we are seeking to grasp is that God is a God of order, not confusion. In the beginning, God's ideals were made perfectly clear. At that time, He provided an orderly place for Adam and Eve to live, as well as order to live by. He provided order to their eating habits. He provided order to their labor. And the Lord even provided order to man's relationship with his wife.

If man stayed within God's predefined boundaries, he was considered successful. If on the other hand he chose to violate God's order, he would be deemed a failure and severely punished. The ideal environment God created for man provided the necessary order for man's success, and within this world God maintained certain expectations and held man accountable to them. These expectations were concrete and objective, unlike the humanistic ideals which permeate the world today.

From the beginning God's actions proclaimed, "I know what's best for man and his wife! I will order their life. I will situate them in a perfect environment. I will give them a perfect nature. I will care for their every need. I will limit them so that their priorities are in order. I will clarify their goals and boundaries. I will do all of this because I love them."

The initial results were very good. God was pleased and glorified by man's actions and attitudes. We know this to be true, for Scripture says, "*And God saw all that He had made, and behold it was very good*" (Gen. 1:31 NAS). God looked upon all of His creation, Adam and Eve included, and was glorified by it; man and his wife were truly successful.

They were successful because in their own simple way they pleased and glorified God. They did so by fully committing all of their hearts, souls, and mights to the object of their affirmation; their Creator. There are many things we may learn from this early account of man's relationship with God, but there are a few which are particularly important.

By looking back to man's creation, we catch a glimpse of God's ideal for all generations. It is important to recognize that just as God set Adam and Eve aside to prepare them for a life of success, He desires that we "allow" the Holy Spirit to set us aside that we might be prepared for lives of spiritual success. God eliminated distractions which might have hindered our ancestors from their walk with God, so we too must identify and rid ourselves of all unnecessary distractions that may deter our walks with God. Therefore, let us strive to focus our entire beings upon the Lord and His will. In doing so we too shall taste the eternal fruit of true success!

3

SUCCESS AFTER THE FALL

TO THE WOMAN HE SAID, "I WILL GREATLY IN-
CREASE YOUR PAINS IN CHILDBEARING"...TO
ADAM HE SAID, ..."THROUGH PAINFUL TOIL YOU
WILL EAT OF IT ALL THE DAYS OF YOUR LIFE IT
WILL PRODUCE THORNS AND THISTLES FOR YOU,
AND YOU WILL EAT THE PLANTS OF THE FIELD.
BY THE SWEAT OF YOUR BROW YOU WILL EAT
YOUR FOOD...."

GENESIS 3:16-19

Adam began his earthly trek with the most ideal environment ever known to mankind; it was designed to maximize his potential for everlasting success. One would think that within such an environment Adam and Eve would have experienced true success. Unfortunately even within a utopian setting, eternal success cannot be taken for granted.

SUCCESS WAS TARNISHED

The temptation and sin of Adam and Eve is one of mankind's most well-known sagas. The account was first recorded by Moses in the book of Genesis chapter three. There we see a short, yet informative account of the events which took place on that fateful day.

The narrative begins with a brief description of the craftiness of the serpent (Gen. 3:1). From other passages of Scripture, we learn that the serpent was Satan himself (John 8:44; 1 John 3:8; Rev. 12:9). Satan, the father of lies and deception, cunningly sought to destroy man's haven of success. The serpent began by deceiving the unsuspecting woman into sin. Satan cleverly baited the woman into questioning the conditions the Lord had established when He forbade man from eating of the *"tree of the knowledge of good and evil"* (Gen. 2:17). Soon after, the woman became the first casualty in the battle of good versus evil. Once the seed of sin was planted in her heart, man ineptly followed (Gen. 3:6). The moment Adam sinned a chain of events began to take place: *"The eyes of both of them were opened, and they realized they were naked"* (Gen. 3:7).

This is a clear indication that their perception of reality had dramatically changed

Prior to sinning, the concept of nakedness was incomprehensible to man and his wife. After the Fall, their perception had changed so drastically that they no longer viewed their nakedness as innocent but rather as something very shameful. The revelation upset them to the point that *"they sewed fig leaves together and made coverings for themselves"* (Gen. 3:7).

Another indication that man's perception had changed was his response to God's presence in the garden. Adam and his wife *"hid from the LORD God among the trees of the garden"* (Gen. 3:8). This is striking in that prior to man's sin, when God sought fellowship with man, interaction was welcome and natural. After the fall, man and his wife fled from God, hoping to avert His attention. Their attempt to hide themselves was absolutely futile, for they were dealing with the Almighty. Thus as a result of man's sin, we see that his perception of reality changed immediately. The man who once felt safe, secure, and content in his home, now understood such things as nakedness, shame, fear, aversion, rationalization, and so forth. The foundation from which he was to base a life of happiness and success was laid to rubble by the violent repercussions emanating from a single godless deed.

MANKIND WAS TARNISHED

The perceptual deviation man initially experienced was only a by-product of a much greater transformation. When God created man, He made him with a perfect and pure nature, one which knew no sin. At the time of Adam's sin, his nature was altered from one of perfection to one of corruption. The corrupt nature was a result of the spiritual death of Adam. The spiritual life, fellowship, and privileges he once enjoyed with God ceased the moment he disobeyed Him. It is for this reason that Adam and Eve hid themselves from God when He attempted to engage in fellowship. The spirit of love and friendship once enjoyed had been corrupted into fear and uncertainty.

MAN'S FOCUS SHIFTED TO SELF

Prior to Satan's presence in the garden, Adam and Eve's relationships were limited to that of God and themselves. This provided the ideal environment for spiritual and intellectual growth. It allowed God to dictate their development as their only concerns were those God placed before them.

Yet even before the Fall, we see Adam and his wife's attention begin to shift from God.

This becomes evident as Eve converses with the serpent. Adam likewise proved himself easily distracted as he quietly observed Eve's conversation. This fatal trend was compounded when Eve partook of the forbidden fruit (Gen. 3:6). All this took place prior to Adam's sin. Thus it is apparent that even before the Fall, man's attention had slowly begun to divert from God. This in and of itself was an important factor in the Fall of man.

Once Adam and Eve were expelled from the garden, man increasingly focused less upon God and more upon himself. This self-centered attitude was later displayed by others such as Cain, Enoch, and Lamech. By the time of Noah's generation, Scripture reports,

> *The Lord saw how great man's wickedness on the earth had become, and that every inclination of the thoughts of his heart was only evil all the time.*
>
> (Gen. 6:5)

Man apart from God focused entirely on himself. He did not seek out God but sought to further a relationship with himself. Furthermore, this has been man's pattern from the Fall onward. Apart from God's intervention, man will never maintain a proper relationship with Him. He may outwardly appear to focus on things other than himself, but inwardly all roads lead back to self.

In the beginning when man was alone with God, the Lord was his only teacher. Man grew and developed in a natural and perfect way under his Father's tutelage. But Adam willfully chose to partake of the forbidden fruit, and in doing so he renounced God as his teacher. At the time of Adam's ill-fated decision, all of mankind, like it or not, was enrolled in the school of hard knocks. No longer would man have the privilege of sitting at the feet of the Creator and learning from Him. Rather, he was now destined to struggle from generation to generation, bungling his way down the path of self-study.

MAN'S LIFE BECAME CONFUSED

As quickly as man was brought into existence by the creative hand of God, he was ushered out of his garden paradise. Adam and Eve found themselves on the outside looking in, and along with their new-found freedom, they discovered that the order and harmony they took for granted while in the garden had greatly dissipated.

Adam and Eve found themselves in a strange and hostile new world. The rhyme and reason were gone. They became confused and misguided. Instead of a beautiful garden sustained by the Creator, the ground demanded tedious labor and was full of thorns and thistles (Gen. 3:17-19). Increasingly, man fell out of sync with God's ways. This is verified by the murder of Abel by his brother Cain (Gen. 4:8). Out of jealousy, we see one brother murder another. Later we see Cain's descendant Lamech also murder out of pride and revenge (Gen. 4:23).

Man's bewilderment and chaos seem to have no boundaries. History is laden with foolish acts; it is a sad tale of the blind leading the blind. Man apart from God aimlessly spends his life chasing the wind, pursuing and reaping success—without success.

A TARNISHED ENVIRONMENT

When God created man, He placed him in an environment which accommodated his every need and provided everything necessary to help him become truly successful in God's eyes. When Adam sinned the environment was no longer perfect, but became tainted along with mankind. This was due to the curse God levied upon His creation. *"Cursed is the ground because of you"* (Gen. 3:17). Because of man the environment suffered greatly. The extent of the distress is not completely evident in Genesis 3, but if we consider the words of the apostle Paul in Romans our understanding of the devastation Adam's sin reaped upon the world becomes clear. Paul says,

> *The creation waits in eager expectation for the sons of God to be revealed. For the creation was subjected to frustration, not by its own choice, but by the will of the one who subjected it, in hope that the creation itself will be liberated from its bondage to decay and brought into the glorious freedom of the children of God. We know that the whole creation has been groaning as in the pains of childbirth right up to the present time.*
>
> (Rom. 8:19-22)

Here we see a world which has been, and continues to be, in a state of shock. When Adam sinned, his wrong-doing influenced much more than his own personal nature. Unfortunately his sin brought havoc upon an entire world and all of mankind for generations to follow. When one contemplates sin's devastation upon the earth, it makes global nuclear warfare look like a mere street fight.

RESULTS OF MAN'S ACTIONS

Despite man's promising beginnings, he displeased and dishonored the Creator. In the beginning God was pleased and glorified by man's actions and attitudes, but once the Devil "came to town" things were never to be the same. Man quickly succumbed to the deceptive ways of Satan. Man had victory in the palm of his hand; he simply needed to be faithful and obedient to God's word. Man did not do the sensible, logical, or moral thing; he chose to disobey.

The repercussions of Adam's sin are experienced to this day. All death, sickness, sorrow, and sin may be traced back to the actions of our first parents. The ripple effect of Adam's sin is tremendous and beyond comprehension. As children of his sad heritage, it is essential we learn from Adam's mistake. We must recognize that all sin finds its origin in self-exultation. The seeds of sin were planted in the heart of Adam the moment he took eyes off God. When man allows his attention to be lured away from the Lord, sin is imminent.

4

SUCCESS AT THE CROSS

FOR IF YOU LIVE ACCORDING TO THE SINFUL NA-
TURE, YOU WILL DIE; BUT IF BY THE SPIRIT YOU
PUT TO DEATH THE MISDEEDS OF THE BODY, YOU
WILL LIVE, BECAUSE THOSE WHO ARE LED BY
THE SPIRIT OF GOD ARE SONS OF GOD. ...NOW IF
WE ARE CHILDREN, THEN WE ARE HEIRS—HEIRS
OF GOD AND CO-HEIRS WITH CHRIST, IF INDEED
WE SHARE IN HIS SUFFERINGS IN ORDER THAT
WE MAY ALSO SHARE IN HIS GLORY.

ROMANS 8:13-14, 17

During the first half of the eighteenth century, well-known Scottish minister Ralph Erskine penned the following words to a gospel sonnet: "Oft earth, and hell, and sin have strove, To rend my soul from God; But everlasting is his love, Seal'd with his Darling's blood."[5] The tender words of Pastor Erskine speak joyously of God's everlasting love for man. To Erskine, the love he had personally experienced was "Seal'd with his Darling's blood." The "Darling" he reverently speaks of is the Son of God, the Lord Jesus Christ.

RESTORED BY CHRIST

In 1 Corinthians 15, while teaching on the resurrection of the dead, Paul contrasts Adam with Christ in several key verses. His comparison reveals what man can be through Christ, over and against what man is in Adam. Paul begins his comparison by pointing out that *"in Adam all die"* (1 Cor. 15:22). Why? Because *"sin entered the world through one man* [Adam], *and death through sin, and in this way death came to all men, because all sinned"* (Rom. 5:12). Through Paul's teaching we learn that "in Adam," *"all have sinned and fall short of the glory of God"* (Rom. 3:23). Thus, all men are under the curse of death, because in their sinfulness they have failed to please or glorify God. Likewise, all men are hopelessly doomed to eternal failure, because in and of themselves they lack the necessary means to overcome the evils of sin's influence.

If Paul were to end his message on this note, we would have nothing but the frighting prospect of eternal punishment. But, thanks to God, the apostle continues *"so in Christ all* [true believers] *will be made alive"* (1 Cor. 15:22). This is possible because

We were therefore buried with him through baptism into death in order that, just as Christ was raised from the dead through the glory of the Father, we too may live a new life. (Rom. 6:4)

Through His death and resurrection, Christ, the "last Adam" provided life (1 Cor. 15:22), and the blessing of His accomplishment has been passed on to all those who are His beloved children. As a result of Christ's faithfulness, man is able to obtain eternal success. Paul joyfully declares, *"thanks be to God! He gives us the victory through our Lord Jesus Christ"* (1 Cor. 15:57). Paul speaks of victory over death and sin. For this reason, Paul is able to resoundingly proclaim, *"Death has been swallowed up in victory. Where, O death, is your victory? Where, O death, is your sting?"* (1 Cor. 15:54-55).

The first Adam experienced a short-lived period of victory in the garden. When he sinned, he forfeited any possibility of achieving a lasting success (Rom. 8:8). The second Adam

experienced permanent victory over sin and
has freely passed the benefits onto His spiritual offspring. He *"humbled himself and became obedient to death—even death on a
cross!"* (Phil. 2:8). Through this obedience, the
Father's wrath was appeased when He gazed
upon the sacrifice of His precious Son. Thus,
by the shedding of His blood and triumph over
the grave, the Lord accomplished that which
man could not do—He fulfilled God's holy law
with perfect obedience and paid the full price
of man's sin. As a result, the restoration of
man is now a reality, and the beacon of eternal
success burns brighter than ever!

As mentioned earlier, man was created
with a pure and sinless nature. Because of
Adam's sin, *every man* is born with a sin nature (Psa. 51:5; Rom. 8:1-11; Eph. 2:1-5),
thereby resulting in eternal punishment. Our
Lord came to this world offering Himself as a
spotless sacrifice for the sins of man. Christ
enabled man to shed the constraints of this
nature, which had held him captive since
birth. Consequently, through God's grace and
the Holy Spirit's divine influence upon the
human heart, man may now live a life of consistent success in Christ.

The reality of this is seen when Paul an-
nounces, *"You, however, are controlled not by*

the sinful nature but by the Spirit" (Rom. 8:9). We are no longer held captive by a nature leading us to eternal ruin, but rather we are free to follow the indwelling Spirit's daily guidance.

The power of sin was broken at the Cross, and man's focus can once again be upon God. In Ephesians 1:18-19, while urging the believers of Ephesus to maintain a deeper walk with Christ, Paul says, *"I pray also that the eyes of your heart may be enlightened in order that you may know the hope to which He has called you."* Here Paul emphasizes that within the heart of every believer, there lies an inner awareness of God, and the things of God.

Before salvation, man's eyes were on self. Once saved, the eyes of man's heart are refocused. The new believer's purpose is to maintain and deepen his focus in such a way as to see less of self, and more of the hope, riches, and power which accompany salvation.

Interestingly enough, man apart from Christ spends his life learning from self and others like him. When man experiences salvation through Christ, the Holy Spirit comes upon and indwells in him. At that time, the Holy Spirit begins to minister to the new believer through the teaching ministry. The

apostle John highlights the teaching function
of the Spirit's ministry when he says,

> *As for you, the anointing you received
> from him remains in you, and you do
> not need anyone to teach you. But as his
> anointing teaches you about all things
> and as that anointing is real, not coun-
> terfeit—just as it has taught you, remain
> in him.* (1 John 2:27)

> *We have not received the spirit of the
> world but the Spirit who is from God,
> that we may understand what God has
> freely given us. This is what we speak,
> not in words taught us by human wis-
> dom but in words taught by the Spirit,
> expressing spiritual truths in spiritual
> words.* (1 Cor. 2:12-13)

The apostle is helping us to understand
the depths of the Holy Spirit's transforming
ministry in the life of the believer. In essence,
he is telling us that the Helper will guide and
direct us through the learning process. In doing so, He will help us understand all that is
necessary to build us up in our faith and the
application of it. For example, on several occasions I have had the opportunity to spend
time teaching the Word to non-believers. Upon

completion of our study, these people had noticeably learned very little. At a later point in time, the Lord graciously saved some of these people. I could clearly see the teaching ministry of the Holy Spirit working in them; to my amazement, people who just a few months earlier could not grasp even the most basic elements of faith were now sharing new insights. Through the Spirit, the Father guides and empowers us in all aspects of our walk.

All who submit to Him will find their lives being reordered by the Spirit. The very essence of this new order is seen in the statement, *"whether you eat or drink or whatever you do, do it all for the glory of God"* (1 Cor. 10:31). When Paul commands the believer to glorify God *"whether you eat or drink,"* he illustrates the extent to which God demands our fullest measure of love and commitment.

We might consider such a command ludicrous. What does eating and drinking have to do with glorifying God? Does God actually observe every meal and drink? With the many concerns each of us face daily, does God really expect this to be a priority? The fact of the matter is that God loves us so much the Bible says, *"the very hairs of your head are all numbered"* (Matt. 10:30). As a result, not one hair shall fall to the ground apart from His will. Is

God concerned with minute details? He most certainly is.

Does He expect His children to be concerned with minute details? Only those details He has commanded us to uphold. The essence of this command is based on God's nature. As His children, we are commanded to be as He is. Thus, when we seek to glorify Him through every aspect of our lives, we are simply emulating Him. In other words, we find ourselves being like God when we concern ourselves with the things God is concerned with. Consequently, if God finds glory in our eating and drinking or in whatever we do, who are we to consider such things unimportant?

As God seeks to reorder our lives through the Holy Spirit, let us never forget that He is thoroughly interested in everything we do. From the top of our heads to the bottom of our feet, in our worship, home, work, and play, God cares. Whether we encounter happiness or sadness, life or death, God cares.

RESULTS OF CHRIST'S ACTIONS

When Adam sinned, he displeased and dishonored his Creator. Since the days of Adam, all men in one way or another have displeased and dishonored the Lord. But our gracious and merciful Father saw fit to send His only Son into a vile world, to die on the cross for the sins of man. When Christ died on the cross, He opened a new chapter in the history of mankind. Prior to His coming, man in and of himself was unable to please or glorify God through his actions. But now, those in Christ, through the empowering of the Holy Spirit, may once again please and glorify the Lord. Prior to Christ's coming, eternal success was far beyond man's reach, but through Christ we can know victory upon victory! Man apart from God could never produce anything of true worth.

Let us now fully commit ourselves to a life of service and success in the Lord Jesus Christ. Through the empowering of the Holy Spirit let us resoundingly praise and glorify the Lord, for He has taken us from the despair and shame of sin into the joy and exultation of eternal salvation. Together let us put our entire focus upon the living God, for He alone is worthy. Likewise, let us rejoice in the fact that through Christ a true and lasting success has been provided at the Cross!

BEACONS OF SUCCESS

A FEW HONEST MEN ARE BETTER THAN
NUMBERS. IF YOU CHOSE GODLY, HONEST MEN TO
BE CAPTAINS OF HORSES, HONEST MEN WILL
FOLLOW.

> OLIVER CROMWELL
> LORD PROTECTOR OF ENGLAND
> —REORGANIZATION OF THE ARMY, 1645

I recall many times as a young boy riding in the car with my family. Sometimes I would notice the brilliance of a powerful searchlight dancing across the sky. The giant beacon would catch my attention and cause me to wonder where it came from and why it was there. Later in life, I realized the beacon was to draw people's attention.

When I think of success, I envision a great beacon casting its light throughout the sky. By its sheer brilliance, it is consistently able to draw people from all walks of life. Why? Because people long to become successful. Today more than ever, people are clamoring to succeed. Some desire it so much they are willing to listen to just about anyone who appears to be successful. This has produced a huge market for books, tapes and seminars specifically dealing with the concept of success.

People desperately want to succeed. As Alexandre Dumas once said, "Nothing succeeds like success."[6] If someone appears to be successful, like a great beacon, he or she will attract a following. The concept is not new; the Bible speaks of two types of success—provisional and eternal.

What is provisional success? It is temporary or transient in nature, here today and gone tomorrow. Provisional success is the culmination of all wealth, privilege, and accomplishment a person has acquired throughout the course of his or her life. It is the exultation of one's self apart from God. It is an outgrowth which will not last beyond the earthly existence of man.

An example of provisional success is seen in Luke 12:13-21. A large crowd had gathered to hear Jesus teach. Suddenly, someone in the crowd demanded Christ to settle a family dispute over an inheritance. Christ refused to act as mediator, and warned the man, *"Watch out! Be on your guard against all kinds of greed; a man's*

*life does not consist in the abundance of his pos-
sessions"* (v. 15).

Why did Christ respond in such a harsh
manner? To understand Christ, we must consider the context. Here was a man standing in
the presence of the very Son of God, with the
privilege of hearing Him share the Word as it
was actually unfolding. Strangely enough, the
only thing he could think of was getting a portion of his brother's inheritance. The Lord's response was not harsh or inappropriate. He
realized that this man was so materialistic that
even though the Messiah Himself was standing
before him, his attitude was not altered in the
least. Jesus continued His rebuke by sharing the
parable of the rich fool:

> *The ground of a certain rich man pro-
> duced a good crop. He thought to him-
> self, "What shall I do? I have no place to
> store my crops." Then he said, "This is
> what I'll do. I will tear down my barns
> and build bigger ones, and there I will
> store all my grain and my goods. And
> I'll say to myself, 'You have plenty of
> good things laid up for many years.
> Take life easy; eat, drink and be merry.'"
> But God said to him, "You fool! This
> very night your life will be demanded*

> *from you. Then who will get what you have prepared for yourself?" This is how it will be with anyone who stores up things for himself but is not rich toward God.* (Luke 12:16-21)

The rich man produced so much excess harvest that he had nowhere to store it. While contemplating the thought of retirement, God chastised him. Later that very night God took his life as promised.

At first glance the parable seems somewhat confusing; it appears as if God was angry because of the rich man's diligence. Several things stand out upon closer examination of the parable. First of all, the rich man hoarded his crops rather than sharing the surplus with the needy (v. 17). From verses 18-19, it appears this had been going on for some time.

Secondly, he lacked a thankful heart. Jesus talks of the farmer's prosperity but says nothing of his thankfulness. The fool made his living from off the land, yet could not see God's hand blessing his endeavors.

Thirdly, the rich fool had an extremely independent attitude. By scanning the parable, we notice many references to himself. Apparently the farmer considered himself the lone entity in this venture. Thus, he consulted only himself when decisions had to be made: God was not included in the equation.

Lastly, the man assumed he had many years to live. But *"God said to him, 'You fool! This very night your life will be demanded from you"* (v. 20).

We might be tempted to condemn the rich man because of his wealth. Yet his sin was based on his priorities not his prosperity. He was seeking a provisional success. He lived for the moment and in doing so denied God. It is for this reason that God said, *"This is how it will be with anyone who stores up things for himself but is not rich toward God"* (v. 21). Is He telling us not to store provisions necessary for our next meal? Or that we should not save for a "rainy day"? What are we to make of Scripture that encourages us to save for the future? Proverbs 6:6-8 says,

> *Go to the ant you sluggard; consider its ways and be wise! It has no commander, no overseer or ruler, yet it stores its provisions in summer and gathers its food at harvest.*

Proverbs 21:20 confirms the point with,

> *In the house of the wise are stores of choice food and oil, but a foolish man devours all he has.*

Jesus is not condemning wise stewardship:
He is condemning a lack of stewardship. Jesus
did not have a problem with the benefit but
the benefactor. The Lord establishes this by
saying, *"anyone who stores up things for himself."* Notice He does not place the emphasis
on the storing up, but rather on the one doing
the storing. Jesus has a problem with anyone
who places something above God.

Another example we might consider is
that of couple Ananias and Sapphira (Acts 5:1-
11). During the church's early days, believers
were selling property to support their fellow
Christians. Ananias and Sapphira sold their
belongings and then pretended to share everything with the apostles, while in reality *"he
kept back part of the money for himself"* (v. 2).
When Peter confronted Ananias in his deception, Scripture says, *"he fell down and died"*
(v. 5). Unaware of what had earlier transpired
with her husband, Sapphira also lied to Peter,
and God struck her down.

The sin Ananias and Sapphira committed
was attempting to deceive the Holy Spirit.
Their motivation was based on greed and self-
ishness. Both the rich farmer and the couple
were withholding that which rightfully belonged to God. In the case of Ananias, his
withholding was small, the deception momen-

tary, and the desire for earthly recognition strong. The rich fool withheld everything and denied God's involvement in his life.

Interestingly enough, God exacted the same punishment upon Ananias and Sapphira for deceitful, half-hearted giving as He did on the rich man who lived a lie and withheld everything. Thus, at any moment, God could rightfully call any of us to account for our sin.

During Christ's Sermon on the Mount, He helps further our understanding of provisional success by saying,

No one can serve two masters. Either he will hate the one and love the other, or he will be devoted to the one and despise the other. You cannot serve both God and Money. (Matt. 6:24)

The two masters are the objects of man's desire. One master is God, the other being anything other than God. Both are like two great beacons in the sky, displaying a power that is able to draw men to themselves. The worldly master finds its power in man's sin nature, while the godly master finds its power in the Cross of Jesus Christ. The prize of the first master is the attainment of temporary human acclaim, whereas the true Master offers the crown of eternal life.

All men and women are born into this world with the desire to pursue worldly success. Men without Christ are slaves to the cravings of temporal success. If this condition is not altered through the Cross of Jesus Christ, eternal failure is certain. When someone becomes a Christian, the Bible promises he becomes a new creature in Christ (2 Cor. 5:17). This is wonderful because it means salvation and the guarantee of eternal success.

Even with the promise of these marvelous gifts, we are continually in the process of becoming more like the Lord. It is for this reason that Scripture encourages us to *"continue to work out your salvation with fear and trembling"* (Phil. 2:12). The apostle Paul likens our spiritual development to the laying and building upon a foundation. He says,

> *If any man builds on this foundation using gold, silver, costly stones, wood, hay or straw, his work will be shown for what it is, because the Day will bring it to light. It will be revealed with fire, and the fire will test the quality of each man's work. If what he has built survives, he will receive his reward. If it is*

> *burned up, he will suffer loss; he himself*
> *will be saved, but only as one escaping*
> *through the flames.* (1 Cor. 3:12-15)

The elements symbolically represent the various things we may build upon the firm foundation we have in Christ. We may either add sound teaching and good works (gold, silver, and costly stones) which will endure an eternity, or something much less (wood, hay, or straw) which will not stand the test of time. Today more than ever, not only are non-Christians pursuing the wood, hay and straw of this world, but many Christians are as well.

The temptation to invest our time and resources seeking to further our own self-interest is always upon us. Everywhere we turn there's a billboard, commercial, or new car sitting in our neighbor's driveway, which can tempt and lure us away from the gold, silver, and precious stones of our faith. Because worldly success is so easy to attain the allurement of it is difficult for the weak to fight off. A few extra hours of overtime, a part-time job for the wife, and before you know it our priorities are out of whack, our families scattered, and we are just like the rich man, tearing down old barns to raise up new ones.

For those of us in the modern church, how might we relate to the wood, hay, and straw Paul spoke of nearly two thousand years ago? For some it might mean having time for your favorite television program or sporting event yet no time for prayer meetings or Sunday School. It might be failing to complete commitments made to the church or fellow Christians. For others, it might mean investing time in a magazine or newspaper but hardly ever picking up the Word of God.

The list could go on and on, but I'm sure you get the point. Ultimately, wood, hay, and straw are anything that stands in the place of God, His Word, or His ministry. The question isn't whether God allows such things; the question is how much of your time and resources are devoted to it? Do you work your life around the Lord, or is the Lord worked around your life?

A grave danger we face is in thinking like the rich man. He thought he knew it all. He was so arrogant he even thought he knew when he was going to die. Thus, foolishly he put off the things of God for the things of this earth. Like so many others, he was dead before he knew what hit him. If you were to stand before Christ this very day and step into the flames of judgment, what would the result be?

Would you come out gloriously bearing gold, silver, and precious stones?

Today is the day to account for what you have and have not done. God says putting it off is foolish. Let us together make certain that our priorities are pleasing to God and that we are not pursuing after a provisional success which amounts to wood, hay, and straw—a success without success!

During the early years of my Christian training, I heard an account of a missionary who ministered ten years in a country dominated by Islam. I remember how perplexed I was when I heard that only three or four people came to Christ during that time. Thus, I made the presumptuous judgment that he could not have been much of a missionary. I did not realize how distorted my view of reality was. I did not fathom the many pressures, obstacles and heartaches missionaries face when attempting to minister in Islamic countries.

Later I realized my unfair estimation of the man's ministry was due to my view of success. As an American, I had been conditioned to appraise success through the distorted grid of a Monopoly game board: those who accumulated the most were the winners and everyone else a loser. As Christians living in America, we often allow our views of success to be influenced more by our culture than by our faith. This is particularly true when it comes to discerning the overall worth and value of things. As Americans we tend to be impressed by numbers, size, external beauty, and so forth. As a result, many Christians prefer large ministries to small ones, numerous conversions to few, and handsome preachers to plain ones.

These things are not inherently evil, but we must recognize that bigger does not always mean better and might does not necessarily mean right. Due to the strong cultural influence, it is extremely important that we sift our view of success through the sieve of God's Word. In doing so, we will find that God does not view success through the narrow framework of the American dream. Success is determined by eternal principles found in God's Word.

Scripture advocates a success which is everlasting and permanent—one which goes beyond the superficialities of cultural ideals. Eternal success finds its culmination in the death and resurrection of the Lord Jesus Christ. Therefore, His disciples find their strength and success in and through Him. The only basis for failure is when someone or something is exalted above Him. Thus, the highest attainment any man may claim is to be a child of God and actively engaged in glorifying Him.

In the gospel of Matthew is the short but revealing parable of the hidden treasure.

> *The kingdom of heaven is like treasure hidden in a field. When a man found it, he hid it again, and then in his joy went and sold all he had and bought that field.* (Matt. 13:44)

Here Jesus establishes the importance and value of pursuing and possessing the kingdom of heaven. He does so by portraying it as a "treasure" which someone hid for safekeeping.

In doing so, Jesus established three essential steps to attaining eternal success. The first step is to **acknowledge**. What must we acknowledge? The "treasure."

I once heard of a man who was browsing through an antique shop. He came across a painting he knew to be of great worth. When he inquired about the price, to his great surprise it was unusually low. Happily, the man gave the dealer the amount requested. Within days the man and his new-found treasure were in the news. Clearly the dealer had failed to recognize the worth of the painting, whereas the man did not. Some people, like the dealer, stumble upon the treasure of God's kingdom yet fail to recognize its worth. This shows that apart from acknowledging the worth of something very special, reaping its benefits are next to impossible!

The second step we are directed to take is to **abandon**. Once the man found the treasure, he *"hid it again, and in his joy went and sold all he had."* He acknowledged the necessity of turning away from that which rightfully belonged to him, for he could not maintain his possessions and secure the treasure as well. It is important to note that, without delay, the man willfully chose to part with everything else in order to secure his heart's desire.

Jesus reiterates the importance of abandonment when He proclaims, *"Whoever finds his life will lose it, and whoever loses his life for my sake will find it"* (Matt. 10:39). When one truly acknowledges the prize, the compulsion to surrender everything flows freely and naturally. The man or woman who truly accepts Jesus as Lord and Savior reacts much like the man who found the treasure. Through the leading of the Holy Spirit, they are compelled to forsake everything in order to claim His kingdom as their own.

If we love our life, or anything more than Christ and His kingdom, it is a sure sign that our loyalty does not belong to Him. An example is when Jesus said to the rich young ruler:

> *If you want to be perfect, go, sell your*
> *possessions and give to the poor, and you*
> *will have treasure in heaven. Then come,*
> *follow me.*   (Matt. 19:21)

The willingness to abandon his wealth in order to follow the Lord was lacking; he in turn forfeited the riches Christ offered. In order to claim the eternal treasure Christ offers, we must be willing to surrender all.

The third and final step we must take in order to grasp eternal success is to **acquire**. The parable indicates that once the man had acknowledged the treasure, he abandoned everything in order to acquire the land on which it rested. Here is a man who set his sights on the object of his passion. He counted the cost of possessing the treasure and joyfully paid it.

Why was he willing to give up everything? Because he knew that he would reap much more than he would sow. He realized that the wealth of the treasure far surpassed his life's possessions. If we gather nothing else from this parable, we must grasp the importance of acquiring the eternal treasure lying before us.

Ultimately, through Christ, the treasure has been paid for. In return we must offer up our most valued possession, our life, to gain His eternal treasure. Why? Because it is absolutely necessary that by faith, we unreservedly buy into a relationship with Christ. To claim ownership without owning is absurd. And part ownership is no ownership!

Each step in the process of securing eternal success plays an important role. Acknowledging starts us on our way, abandoning helps us count the cost, and acquiring consummates our ownership. Once we acquire our treasure, many of us are tempted to leave it buried in the ground and do nothing with it. Approaching our new-found wealth from this perspective is not pleasing to God. He never intended for the treasure to lie dormant, but rather He wants us to use it in such a way as to "*add to it.*"

In the Sermon on the Mount, Jesus discusses the discipline of amassing treasures:

> *Do not store up for yourselves treasures on earth, where moth and rust destroy, and where thieves break in and steal. But store up for yourselves treasures in heaven, where moth and rust do not destroy, and where thieves do not break in*

and steal. For where your treasure is,
there your heart will be also.

(Matt. 6:19-21)

By carefully reading through the entire
passage, we notice that Christ's directive is
bathed within the context of pursuing righteous deeds. The Lord contrasts between those
who make a public display of their deeds with
those who perform them in private. Jesus
touches upon such basic things as giving (vv.
2-4), prayer (vv. 5-13), forgiveness (vv. 14-15),
and fasting (vv. 16-18). With this backdrop
Christ makes it clear that each of us has the
opportunity to store treasures on earth (v. 19)
or in heaven (v. 20).

If we opt for earthly treasures we have put
our trust in something fleeting. On the other
hand, if we pursue heavenly treasures, we
store up riches that last an eternity. Heavenly
treasures are righteous deeds done for the
purpose of glorifying God. As mentioned earlier, no matter what we do—eat, drink, pray,
or fast—it must be with the intent of glorifying God. This sacred ambition stands at the
very heart of Christianity! When contemplating our sacred objective, it is important to note
that there is no endeavor more worthwhile
than to please and glorify the Lord.

The reality of this fact is seen in the diary of young David Brainerd, a missionary to the American Indians during the mid-1800's. Pondering God's "goodness and mercy" he wrote,

> I longed to be perfectly holy that I might not grieve a gracious God, who will continue to love, notwithstanding His love is abused! I longed for holiness more for this end than I did for my own happiness' sake. Yet this was my greatest happiness, never more to dishonor, but always to glorify, the blessed God.[7]

Truly, our dear brother understood the reality of the Christian experience. In the most humble manner possible, he offered his life as a living sacrifice for the purpose of glorifying God. In his pursuit, he stored many heavenly treasures.

As with brother David, we too must find our happiness and fulfillment in glorifying God. For as we grasp this reality, we shall dwell in the light of eternal success.

Jesus concludes His directive by proclaiming, *"For where your treasure is, there your heart will be also"* (v. 21). In near poetic fashion, Jesus establishes a clear-cut standard for determining the essence of a person's loyalty. If, and only if, you are pursuing eternal treasures, then your loyalty is aligned with God Himself.

Jesus leaves no room for a middle ground; we are either pursuing God or pursuing something else. The choice is ours. Before us shine two great beacons—one provisional, the other eternal. The beacon of provisional success is temporary, here today and gone tomorrow. It is like the wood, hay, and straw that will be consumed by the fire of judgment. It is a treasure chest bearing no treasure. On the other hand, the beacon of eternal success is everlasting and stored safely in heaven with our Lord. It is like gold, silver, and precious stones which will not be consumed by the fire. It is a treasure which is unsurpassed and full of eternal wealth. The choice is ours! No one can serve two masters. Where does your treasure lie?

ONE LIFE TO LIVE

ONE LIFE TO LIVE! BUT ONE, BUT ONE!
AND LO! THE HOURS ARE GOING,
THE DAYS AND WEEKS, THE MONTHS
AND YEARS,
A CURRENT SWIFTLY FLOWING.

ONE LIFE TO LIVE! WHAT SHALL IT BE,
FOR WINNING OR FOR LOSING?
IT FALLS TO ME, AND NONE BESIDE,
THE SOLEMN RIGHT OF CHOOSING.

ONE LIFE TO LIVE, AND THEN TO GO
WHERE LIFE GOES ON, UNENDING,
AND WHAT THAT OTHER LIFE SHALL BE,
ALL ON THIS LIFE DEPENDING!

ONE LIFE TO LIVE! I FEEL THE URGE
TO EARNEST, HIGH ENDEAVOR,
FOR WHAT I AM AND WHAT I DO,
WHILE HERE, MUST BE FOREVER!

ONE LIFE TO LIVE! NO TIME HAVE I
FOR DALLYING OR DREAMING,
I MUST BE LIVING AT MY BEST,
THE PRECIOUS HOURS REDEEMING.[8]

Reverend Thomas O. Chisholm

FOUNDATIONAL TRUTHS

REMAIN IN ME, AND I WILL REMAIN IN YOU. NO
BRANCH CAN BEAR FRUIT BY ITSELF; IT MUST
REMAIN IN THE VINE. NEITHER CAN YOU BEAR
FRUIT UNLESS YOU REMAIN IN ME.

JOHN 15:4

Within every field of study exist foundational truths which guide our understanding of a particular topic. The concept of biblical success, like any other subject, maintains truths which shape and direct our understanding. It is impossible to fully appreciate God's view of success apart from examining His truths. Therefore, we will briefly consider several fundamental truths.

While studying the history of success, we saw that in Eden, God-centered success initially reigned. Unfortunately, the success which man experienced was tarnished as a result of the Fall. Thousands of years later, success once again became possible through the death and resurrection of Jesus Christ. The success we find through Christ may be broken down into three phases: conception, cultivation, and consummation. To aid us in our understanding, we will examine each phase as seen through the life of the apostle Paul.

CONCEPTION

Let's begin by taking a look at the conception phase, which takes place at the point of spiritual rebirth. When someone becomes a child of God, they not only go from darkness to light, but from spiritual failure to spiritual success. The success we experience is not based on anything we have done but rather on those things which were accomplished by Jesus during His earthly ministry. As His disciples, we find our success in Him, through Him, and because of Him. Thus, we may be assured that there is no greater success than to become a child of the King.

Of all the characters portrayed throughout Scripture, the life of the apostle Paul most clearly illustrates the conception of spiritual success. In 1 Timothy 1:13, we are able to survey the essence of Paul's disposition prior to his conversion to Christianity. Paul says, "I *was once a blasphemer and a persecutor and a violent man.*" The blasphemy he speaks of was based on his rejection of Christ as the Son of God. He displayed this by means of severe persecution and violence directed toward the church. Paul acknowledges this by saying,

> *I put many of the saints in prison, and when they were put to death, I cast my vote against them. Many a time I went from one synagogue to another to have them punished, and I tried to force them to blaspheme* (Acts 26:10-11)

To the church of Jesus Christ, Paul was as the Devil himself. From his innermost being he poured forth hate and death upon those who aligned themselves with Christ. He was a one-man wrecking crew, seeking to demolish the church. Who would have ever imagined that this "devil" of a man would one day submit to the lordship of Jesus Christ? But the Bible tells us that is exactly what happened.

The miraculous transformation of Paul began as he neared the city of Damascus. Christ stopped him dead in his tracks saying, "*Saul, Saul, why do you persecute me?*" Paul,

in his confusion, asked, *"Who are you, Lord?"*
The voice responded, *"I am Jesus, whom you
are persecuting. Now get up and go into the
city, and you will be told what you must do"*
(Acts 9:4-6).

There on the road to Damascus, Paul was
humbled, blinded, and introduced to the
Author of eternal success. He immediately fell
into a state of mental and emotional shock. In
one traumatic moment, Paul realized that he
had been wasting his life pursuing temporary
success, without true success. For many years,
Paul was convinced that true success could be
grasped through the legalistic pursuit of
Pharisaism. In one brief yet astounding encounter, the Lord showed Paul how wrong he
was. Like a blast of lightening shattering a
figure of a mammoth tree, Jesus decimated
Paul's view of success by proclaiming, *"I am
Jesus, whom you are persecuting"* (Acts 9:5).

Because of the reality of Christ's presence
and the forcefulness of His assertion, Paul
found himself intellectually, emotionally, and
spiritually naked before the risen Christ.
Rather than fighting the inevitable, Paul forfeited the provisional success he had amassed
through Judaism. Hence, he experienced true
success the moment he embraced the Way, the
Truth, and the Life!

As in the case of all those who truly accept Christ as Savior, Paul did not seek out Christ, but rather Christ met him. It was Jesus who said, *"No one can come to me unless the Father who sent me draws him"* (John 6:44). If anyone ever understood the drawing power of God, it was Paul. He was not only drawn but stopped and redirected by the Divine presence.

When I think of Paul's experience, I'm reminded of the effect a magnet has upon metallic objects. When an object is placed within the magnetic field, it is drawn and firmly secured by the magnet. This is the result of the magnetic force drawing the object to itself. Those who experience the new birth, in similar fashion, are drawn by the Holy Spirit to faith in Jesus Christ. Like the metallic object, once we have been drawn, we are firmly secured by Him. Eternal success is ours through Christ.

The success we find in Christ assures us of forgiveness, cleansing, and the ability to overcome sin. We are given a new nature and the indwelling of the Holy Spirit within us. Through Christ, the riches of eternal success are showered upon everyone at the moment of spiritual conception. For those in Christ there is much reason to rejoice. Together, as with a host of angels, let us sing, "Oh, what a victory! Oh, what a blessing! Oh, what a Savior!"

CULTIVATION

The second phase of success is cultivation. The word "cultivate" bears special significance to those in the agricultural world. The term is most often used in relation to the process of growing plants and vegetation. As we consider the process of spiritual cultivation, we will consider three specific details regarding it: the preparation, growth, and nurture of a believer.

PREPARATION

The first aspect of cultivation is that of preparation. Before one is able to sow, the ground must first be prepared. This is done by tilling the ground which loosens the soil and dislodges weeds and other undesirable objects. Just as farmers must prepare the ground to sow seed, as Christians we must also be spiritually prepared.

We see an example of this during Paul's encounter with Christ. Once Jesus had corrected Paul's attitude regarding His deity, He commanded Paul saying, *"Now get up and go into the city, and you will be told what you must do"* (Acts 9:6). Jesus sent Paul to a location where he would begin to prepare for his life of service. Because Paul was left blinded by his encounter, his associates had to lead him to the house of Judas in the city of Damascus (Acts 9:11). There Christ would send a disciple named Ananias to restore his sight and impart the Spirit (Acts 9:17-18).

During the time Paul waited on the Lord for guidance, what was he doing? Was he resting after his traumatic experience or perhaps mourning over the loss of his sight? Jesus never mentioned to Paul whether his vision would be restored. Practically speaking, he had no way of knowing whether his condition was temporary or permanent. From a human perspective, Paul could have focused entirely on his loss, and therefore responded with depression, anger, or even hatred. Once Paul arrived at Judas' house, Scripture says, *"For three days he was blind, and did not eat or drink anything"* (Acts 9:9).

Did Paul refuse to eat and drink because of depression, anger, or hatred? Could he have been fasting? If he were fasting, was it as a result of the trauma forced upon him or was it by his own free will? When Jesus directed Ananias to go to Paul, He identified the crux of Paul's activity. At that time, Jesus told Ananias that Paul was praying (Acts 9:11). Thus, Paul refrained from eating in order to focus on God. Paul's response to his circumstances tells us a great deal about his attitude and motivation. Rather than turning away from God, he turned to Him. Instead of rejecting that which he could not comprehend, by faith he sought further insight through prayer.

During this very confusing time, why did Paul choose to pray? Because the Holy Spirit led him to. For what reason? In order to prepare him for that which was to come. Even before the messenger came with healing and the filling of the Spirit, God began to prepare the apostle.

Times of preparation are not limited solely to apostles or great men and women of God. It is a ministry which the Holy Spirit imparts to all true believers. More often than not, the Spirit leads us to a Bible-believing church where the Word of God is faithfully preached and taught. At times, depending on the circumstances, God may bring a more mature believer into our life to lead us in the right direction. For many, Christian books, radio, and television have been a source of initial preparation. Regardless of the avenue, the desired result is the same in every case; God wants us to move from a time of initial preparation to that of true growth. Why? Because stagnate immaturity lacks the approval of God.

GROWTH

The second aspect of cultivation is growth. Once the ground has been prepared, it is then ready to accept seed. With the seed, comes the potential for growth. The new believer is much like freshly tilled soil; while it might be prepared, if the Word is not sown, growth is impossible. It is for this reason we are encouraged to regularly sit under the preaching and teaching ministries of God's Word.

Paul, unlike other new believers, had a storehouse of knowledge and understanding regarding the Scriptures. Thus, to some degree he could rely on all he had learned prior to his conversion. Even though Paul knew much about the Old Testament, like soil with new seed, he needed to be watered.

Shortly after his conversion, he *"spent several days with the disciples in Damascus"* (Acts 9:19). Undoubtedly, he absorbed large sums of knowledge regarding Jesus. We see proof of this in his ability to *"preach in the synagogues"* (Acts 9:20) shortly after accepting Christ. The fact that Paul began to preach is evidence that he was growing. For as the Lord said, *"by their fruit you will recognize them"* (Matt. 7:20). Paul clearly bore healthy fruit. In a very short time he grew to the point of baffling the Jews *"by proving that Jesus is the Christ"* (Acts 9:22). He even had a group of followers which he most likely discipled himself (Acts 9:25).

Following Paul's lead, we must pursue the seed of the Word and the "holy water" which causes growth. Like the parched ground, we must thirst for the Word of God and then apply it to our lives. Before God we are responsible for our own growth. If we fail to grow and develop in maturity, we have no one to blame but ourselves. We must make certain that we are continuously partaking of God's Word. He has graciously blessed us by providing His Word, teachers, preachers, disciplers, as well as thousands of books, tapes, videos, seminars, conferences, and so forth, to encourage growth. He has certainly done His part. It is up to us to bear our end of the commitment.

NURTURING

The third and final aspect of cultivation is nurturing. The act of nurturing is dependent on life in a plant. You cannot nurture something that is dead. To nurture is to promote the growth and development of something that is already alive and exhibiting signs of growth. The believer in Christ must be nurtured from immaturity to maturity.

In the parable of the vine and the branches, Jesus establishes the importance of nurturing by saying,

> *I am the true vine, and my Father is the gardener. He cuts off every branch in me that bears no fruit, while every branch that does bear fruit he prunes so that it will be even more fruitful.* (John 15:1-2)

One element of the nurturing process is **pruning**. The purpose of pruning is to thin out a plant in such a way as to promote increased growth. The Lord states that the Father, like a gardener, prunes healthy fruit-bearing Christians to help them produce more fruit. This is done through correction and discipline. Both help to reveal and remove those things that do not promote growth.

Along with pruning, God **waters** and **fertilizes** us as well. A few years ago I purchased a "Spark-Ling Ivy" plant for my office. After caring for the plant for about one year, I noticed that many of the leaves were turning yellow and dying. I could not figure out what was wrong with the plant until I read the back side of the instruction card I had received with it. As I read through the card, I noticed that I was supposed to fertilize the plant every other month. I had not fertilized the plant since buying it. Needless to say, after a few months of proper care, the plant began to recover.

Christians need to be regularly watered and fertilized by the Bible, prayer, fellowship, and so on. If these essentials are lacking, we will not grow. Like my plant, we will not flourish but fade. God has given us His Word and His body not to be a bother but a blessing. To the degree to which we partake of these things, we allow the Spirit to nurture us spiritually.

As Paul achieved new levels of growth, we see God sought to further it, so He directed Paul to leave Damascus and head to Arabia for a time of spiritual nurturing (Gal. 1:17). Just as God set Paul aside for a time of spiritual nurturing, we too must seek our own daily "Arabia." During this time, we ought to meditate upon God's Word and commune with Him in prayer. As His children, we must have a time in which God may speak softly to our hearts or forcefully rebuke us for our foolishness. A quiet time with God is one of the most beneficial ways to partake of the spiritual nurturing He desires for us all.

The ministry of preparation, growth, and nurturing are vital to the development and success of any true believer. The initial success we find in Christ must be complimented by spiritual cultivation through the ministry of the Holy Spirit. We must keep ourselves from becoming lax in this lifelong commitment, while striving to promote success by glorifying God through the ministry of cultivation.

CONSUMMATION

The last phase we must consider is the consummation of the believer. This is the culmination of everything we are and shall be in Christ. Paul refers to the outset of this great and wonderful period by saying

> *We will not all sleep, but we will all be changed—in a flash, in the twinkling of an eye, at the last trumpet. For the trumpet will sound, the dead will be raised imperishable, and we will be changed.*
> (1 Cor. 15:51-52)

The change Paul was anticipating is the transformation all believers will undergo at the time of Christ's return. The dead and living will experience *"the redemption of our bodies"* (Rom. 8:23). In essence, we will take on glorious resurrection bodies and become like our Lord (Phil. 3:21). We may also look forward to entering into our eternal citizenship

(Phil. 3:20), reigning with Christ (2 Tim. 2:12), the wedding supper of the Lamb Christ Jesus (Rev. 19:6-9), and many other great and wonderful privileges. Moreover we will no longer suffer the frailties of our earthly bodies, contend with sin and death (1 Cor. 15:54-57), or be held captive by the misery and failure of a godless world because God has

> *Raised us up with Christ and seated us with him in the heavenly realms in Christ Jesus, in order that in the coming ages he might show the incomparable riches of his grace.* (Eph. 2:6-7)

Truly, this is the great and glorious consummation we joyously anticipate as believers in Christ. Our triumphant future is the light which guides us through the darkness of this hour. Let us be thankful for the new birth we have found in Christ. Let us labor diligently in cultivating fruit for our Lord. And let us find hope and happiness in the end time consummation which awaits us. Scripture says, *"we will be with the Lord forever!"* (1 Thess. 4:17).

At the heart of all true success, is God-centered obedience. Essentially, true obedience is the willful alignment of an individual with God's Word. It is absolutely necessary that such an

alignment be totally motivated by a love for God
and His Word. In God's eyes, obedience goes far
beyond external application of biblical principles.

Jesus made this very clear when He said,

> *You have heard that it was said, "Do not
> commit adultery." But I tell you that
> anyone who looks at a woman lustfully
> has already committed adultery with her
> in his heart.* (Matt. 5:27-28)

In the Old Testament, God commanded
the people to remain sexually pure. Many attempted to obey the command by physically
refraining from acts of adultery. Yet Christ
knew the condition of their hearts and realized
that some were keeping the law outwardly,
while ignoring it inwardly.

The Lord discharged such thinking by
linking man's actions to his thoughts. In doing
so, it became evident that true obedience must
go far beyond man's outward behavior. To
Christ, our actions are nothing more than an
outward sign of an inward reality. From His
perspective, actions are merely an indication of
our inner motivation and heart's attitude.
Thus, if someone looks upon a woman with
lustful eyes, God perceives the act as an outgrowth of a heart motivated by sinful adultery.

It is for this reason Jesus encourages us to view obedience not through man's limited perspective, but through God's vantage point.

Unfortunately, man in his frailty seeks to evade God's perspective. Consequently, every time he equates inward sin with hidden sin, and hidden sin with secluded sin, he finds himself opposing God. There is no amount of pretending or evasion which will help us escape accountability. God has set His standards and demands that each of us align ourselves accordingly. To do otherwise is to mock His divine presence. To God obedience is everything!

Our obedience, or lack of it, is a strong indication of the type of relationship we have with Him. Jesus said, *"by their fruit you will recognize them"* (Matt. 7:20). The fruit He spoke of are deeds performed either to glorify God or to please self. The quality of a man's fruit originates in his heart. If we are motivated by the Spirit, the potential to produce godly fruit is present. On the other hand, if we are motivated by self, our fruit will lack godly approval.

Because the principle of obedience is foundational to the concept of eternal success, the prophet Samuel once said, *"To obey is better than sacrifice"*(1 Sam. 15:22). When speaking of obedience, he was referring to the sort of obedience that is God-centered in nature. Such obedience is motivated by the Holy Spirit and finds its purpose in pleasing and honoring God.

SELF-CENTERED SACRIFICE

Kings Saul and David illustrate the contrast between obedience and self-centeredness. For the majority of his reign, Saul was motivated by self-centeredness. David actively pursued God-centered obedience. As we seek to better understand the difference between the two pursuits, let us do so by means of Saul's and David's examples.

When I think of the rise and fall of men, the single biblical account which saddens my heart more than any other is that of King Saul. Saul stands as a graphic example of success and failure rolled up in one tragic picture. Saul is introduced as an *"impressive young man without equal among the Israelites"* (1 Sam. 9:2). He was of such a humble character that when Samuel sought to make him king, Saul hid himself among the baggage (1 Sam. 10:22). He did not immediately become prideful or arrogant, and was even willing to forgive those who disrespected him and his authority

(1 Sam. 10:27; 11:12-13). During the course of Saul's reign, something drastically changed. The young man who initially showed such promise, took his eyes off the Lord. Through Saul's example, we see a clear picture of self-centered sacrifice and the effect it has upon God and His Word. Even though the ramifications are numerous, for the purpose of our study, we will touch upon only three of the outgrowths attributed to this sin.

THE HALTING OF GOD'S WORD

The first outgrowth of self-centeredness is halting the progress of God's Word. This is a by-product of sinful choices or actions which may occur in the lives of those claiming to be believers. Every time God makes His Word known to us, we have a choice to follow or disregard it. If we obey His Word, regardless of the outcome, we are assured of the Lord's favor. If we disregard His Word, we have set ourselves in direct opposition to His will.

On several occasions during Saul's life, he had the opportunity to stand firm in his faith and further the cause of God. We see one such example when Saul was commanded to wait at Gilgal for a period of seven days, at which time Samuel would come and offer sacrifices to God and instruct him as to the Lord's leading (1 Sam. 10:8). Saul went to Gilgal, as commanded, and waited the seven days. However, because the Philistines were threatening to attack Saul and his army, he failed to wait for Samuel and offered the burnt offering on his own (1 Sam. 13:8-10). At first glance we might be tempted to believe Saul had no other choice than to offer the burnt offering to God. Scripture tells us,

> *The Philistines assembled to fight Israel, with three thousand chariots, six thousand charioteers, and soldiers as numerous as the sand on the seashore. They went up and camped at Micmash, east of Beth Aven. When the men of Israel saw that their situation was critical and that their army was hard pressed, they hid in caves and thickets, among the rocks, and in pits and cisterns. Some Hebrews even crossed the Jordan to the land of Gad and Gilead. Saul remained at Gilgal, and all the troops with him were quaking with fear. He waited seven days, the time set by Samuel; but Samuel did not come to Gilgal, and Saul's men began to scatter.* (1 Sam. 13:5-8)

The king clearly found himself in a very difficult situation. The enemy was assembled and ready to fight. They had superior numbers, weapons, and training. His army was in the process of fleeing or hiding. The seven-day waiting period had ended, and Samuel was nowhere in sight. Humanly speaking, what was Saul to do? His back was to the wall. It would have taken a miracle to get him out of this mess.

Sadly, Saul did not wait on the Lord. When things became really difficult, oddly enough, he turned away from God's Word in order to seek out the Lord's favor (1 Sam. 13:12). Foolishly, Saul believed he could ignore God's Word yet somehow still gain His blessing.

This was ridiculous because outward acts of self-righteousness will never substitute for obedience to God's Word. If we are ever to gain God's favor, it will be as a result of submitting to His Word, not by slipping past it. The king also found himself opposing God when he chose to offer up the burnt offering, for he usurped a responsibility reserved for Samuel. Saul was not a priest, Samuel was. Saul was not commissioned to go to Gilgal and offer the burnt offering, Samuel was. Saul set his eyes on the Philistines, on his overwhelmed army, and on the prospect of Samuel's arrival. He set his eyes on everything but the revealed Word of God. The result was that he became a stumbling block to the progress of God's Word.

The moment Saul turned from obeying God's Word, God turned from Saul. When Samuel arrived at Gilgal, he reproved Saul by saying,

> *You acted foolishly. You have not kept the command the LORD your God gave you; if you had, he would have established your kingdom over Israel for all time. But now your kingdom will not endure; the LORD has sought out a man after his own heart.* (1 Sam. 13:13-14)

King Saul impeded God's plan for him and proved his spiritual character lacked the necessary elements to pass the kingly torch on to the Messiah. Once Samuel finished rebuking Saul, there was no need to sacrifice burnt or fellowship offerings, and—more significantly—no need to share God's direction. There is no sitting on the fence in your relationship with God. Jesus' words are recorded in Matthew 12:30 *"He who is not with me is against me."*

THE HUMANIZING OF GOD'S WORD

The second result of self-centeredness is when someone adds to or subtracts from His revealed Word. Scripture tells us that this is an act which is detestable to God (Prov. 19:9; 28:9). Perhaps the most clear-cut example from Saul's life is seen in 1 Samuel 15. God sent Saul to war with the Amalekites and gave him special instructions through Samuel regarding the execution of his campaign against the sinful tribe. Saul opted to ignore part of them, which nullified the good of those he did obey. The grievous sin Saul committed began the moment he decided to devalue God's Word by changing it.

As is so often the case, God's Word was corrupted not by some ignorant pagan but by one of His chosen servants. Like Saul, far too often those who claim to be Christians are guilty of humanizing God's Word. Rather than focusing on His Word and carefully carrying out every detail, we pick and choose what we will or will not obey. This is foolishness for God has never given any man the right to ignore His Word. To do so is to place ourselves above God!

HUMBLING OF GOD'S WORD

The third and final outgrowth we will consider is the humbling of God's Word. This is brought about as a result of someone directly or indirectly minimizing the importance of the Lord's Word. Because the Bible is divinely inspired, without error, and the standard all true believers must live by, when we depreciate it by our example, we encourage others to do likewise (Mal. 3:13-16).

On several occasions Saul willfully chose to minimize the importance of God's Word. As a result his sin came to fruition when a giant of a man named Goliath was allowed to mock and defy God by harassing Saul and his army. This dreadful scene occurred because Saul chose to minimize God's Word in his life. Consequently, because of his rebelliousness, when Saul needed God's help, God was unavailable.

The fear and anguish that developed from this incident are reflected in the words "*Saul and all the Israelites were dismayed and terrified*" (1 Sam. 17:11). Saul and his men's example was so noticeable that even Goliath realized the shallowness of their faith. This ultimately led to the humbling of God's Word. For forty days Goliath, a single pagan soldier, mocked the Lord and His army. Oh, how it must grieve God to hear the taunts of a pagan world mocking Him and His Word. And for what reason? Like Saul, far too many of us are concerned more with self than upholding the integrity of our Lord and His Word.

What about you? Where do you stand? Have you been living out the life of Saul? Have you been offering self-centered sacrifices to God? Have you been humanizing God's Word by altering it to fit your desires? Have you humbled it by your actions? Have you halted God's Word in your life by ignoring it altogether? True obedience is seen through the willful alignment of an individual with the Word of God. As with Saul, each of us is given the choice as to which path to follow.

GOD-CENTERED OBEDIENCE

In reading through the Old Testament, we see many examples of men and women who strove to please God through obedience. One man who spent his life pursuing a God-centered obedience was King David. No matter what the task or situation, the focal point of David's life was to please and glorify God. He was by no means a perfect man, yet he pursued a God-centered obedience. As a result of his pursuit, we see three outcomes displayed.

HEARING GOD'S WORD

Have you ever been involved in a conversation where you listened to someone but did not pay attention to what was being said? Perhaps you were daydreaming or had something else on your mind. Often people listen to someone without actually hearing a single word said. This not only happens when we discuss things with others but may also occur when God has something to say to us.

One of the great disappointments preachers and teachers experience is sharing a message that people do not hear with their hearts. Often times, God blesses us in spite of our neglect, yet He always desires hearts that are spiritually ready to receive His Word. Such preparedness is found in a consistent and daily walk with Him.

King David, being a man after God's own heart, very seldom struggled with this problem. When God spoke, David was attentive! Whether God was sharing good news, bad news, or even revealing sin, David was ready to hear God's Word. Why? Because he truly loved and respected God. To David, God's Word was a lamp to his feet and a light on his path.

An example of this is seen when David spoke to the prophet Nathan regarding the building of the temple. David, wanting very much to honor God, said to Nathan, *"Here I am, living in a palace of cedar, while the ark of the covenant of the LORD is under a tent"* (1 Chron. 17:1). David felt that he was receiving better treatment than the ark, which symbolized the presence of the Lord. He sought Nathan's advice concerning the building of the temple to house the ark. Nathan replied saying, *"Whatever you have in mind, do it, for God is with you"* (1 Chron. 17:2).

David, having gone through the proper channels, seemed to receive permission to build the temple. Interestingly enough, Scripture tells us that *"the word of God came to Nathan"* (v. 3) commanding him to tell David,

> *You are not the one to build me a house to dwell in...I will raise up your offspring to succeed you, one of your sons, and I will establish his kingdom. He is the one who will build a house for me, and I will establish his throne forever.*
> (1 Chron. 17:4, 11-12)

Talk about a slap in the face! Here David was willing to spend his time, energy, and a phenomenal sum of money to build a beautiful temple to honor the Lord, yet God flatly rejected his love offering. What was David to do? One day he seemed to have permission, the next he did not. This certainly could have caused a great deal of bewilderment and even depression within him.

He could not build the temple, but his son could. Why? David later said that God told him that he could not build the temple because, "[he had] *shed much blood and [had] fought many wars*" (1 Chron. 22:8). God's reasoning is most interesting. David could not build the temple because he was a man of war and bloodshed. But who commissioned David to fight those wars? God did! So in essence, David could not pursue his heart's desire because he had been faithful in carrying out God's previous commands.

Knowing all the facts, how did David choose to respond? He listened to what the prophet had to say and heard with his heart. Humanly speaking, he could have become outraged or questioned God's fairness. He could have stubbornly closed his ears and refused to hear God's Word, but he did not. Why was he willing to receive the Word? Because by faith he realized that God was perfectly just in all His dealings.

HEEDING GOD'S WORD

There are many people who are willing to hear and interact with the Word of God, even if they do not like what it is saying. But there are few who will heed the Word if it goes contrary to their liking. The true man or woman of God hears and then heeds God's Word, regardless of the cost. Scripture tells us that:

> *David said, "My son Solomon is young and inexperienced, and the house to be built for the LORD should be of great magnificence and fame and splendor in the sight of all the nations. Therefore I will make preparations for it." So David made extensive preparations before his death. Then he called for his son Solomon and charged him to build a house for the LORD, the God of Israel.*
>
> (1 Chron. 22:5-6)

The Lord commanded David not to build the temple, and he honored the Lord's will. Not only did he honor the Lord's desire, but he did everything possible to encourage and promote God's plan. The king could have obeyed in a stubborn and begrudging manner or, childishly felt if he could not build the temple, no one could. Even though the privilege was passed on to the king's son, it would be naive to automatically assume David would encourage and support his son. Throughout history, there have been many cases of fathers jealously withholding their support.

How was it possible David could allow his dream to slip through his fingers? Because he understood his place and role before God. He accepted the fact that he was nothing more than one member of God's "team" and that the Lord was the Coach. David was grateful just to be on the team.

David's attitude is sorely missing in our churches today. In 1 Samuel 15:29 it says, *"he who is the Glory of Israel does not lie or change his mind; for he is not a man, that he should change his mind."* If you are one who has rebelliously refused to heed God, do not hold your breath hoping He will change. He will never change because His wisdom and righteousness are complete! Mighty King David heard and heeded God's Word. Are you doing the same?

HONORING GOD'S WORD

There are many people who claim the name of Christ and act as if they honor His Father's Word. Yet, if they fail to hear and heed God's Word, it is impossible to honor it! The Lord of the universe is not honored by sin or half-heartedness. We saw through Saul's example that minimizing God's Word, however slight, is very distasteful to Him.

Most certainly, King David understood the importance of hearing and heeding God's Word. As a result, he knew the only way he would be able to truly honor the Lord was through God-centered obedience. To do otherwise was to fall short of His revealed will. Even though David fell short on a few occasions, his life overall was a fabric of events knitted together in a God-honoring manner. David honored God's Word when he faithfully protected his father's sheep from a lion and a bear (1 Sam. 17:34-36). David honored God's Word when, by faith, he did the impossible by defeating Goliath (1 Sam. 17:49). David honored God's Word when he chose to spare King Saul's life (1 Sam. 24:10; 26:12). David honored God's Word when he went to war with the enemies of God (2 Sam. 8:1-15).

Time and time again, David put his own life in jeopardy. Why? Because he desperately wanted to honor the Lord by his actions and life. David understood that God knew his every thought and feeling. Thus, he diligently sought to honor the Lord with a heart motivated by love and respect for Him. As we reflect on Saul's and David's lives, it is essential to discern which example we are following and which one should be in our future. Just as Saul became an enemy of God and His Word, anyone who ignores or minimizes His Word follows in the footsteps of Saul.

If you have been offering up self-centered sacrifices, I pray that this very moment you repent and turn to God. For if you refuse, you too will one day hear the words Samuel spoke to Saul: *"You have rejected the word of the LORD, and the LORD has rejected you"* (1 Sam. 15:26).

On the other hand, if you have been pursuing a life of God-centered obedience, then you are following David's example and living a life of true success. To obey is better than sacrifice, but obedience is only as real as the consistency and submission that accompany it. This very moment the Lord is calling each of us to a life of obedience. By

His grace, we may pursue a God-centered obedience or settle for a self-centered sacrifice. The choice is ours. God is saying to each of us, "Hear My Word, heed My Word, and honor My Word, that your life may be complete in Me."

TRUE GREATNESS

There is an old saying, "Who can refuse a mother's plea?" We have difficulty ignoring a mother's plea because of the emotional ties we each have to our own mothers. During criminal trials, defense attorneys have used this to their advantage by encouraging a mother to plead on behalf of her son or daughter. This manipulative tool can be a very powerful weapon in the hands of the right person.

Something similar took place during Jesus' ministry here on earth. One day, shortly after Christ had predicted His death, Salome, the mother of James and John, said to Jesus, *"Grant that one of these two sons of mine may sit at your right and the other at your left in your kingdom"* (Matt. 20:21). Clearly, the wife of Zebedee understood the persuasive influence of a mother's charm. By her request, she acknowledged Christ as Lord and King of the universe. She therefore understood that He must sit on the highest throne of honor in His heavenly kingdom. Whoever sat to His immediate right and left held the next highest seats of honor and authority. It is no wonder the other apostles were indignant with this request (Matt. 20:24).

Based on her actions, it is safe to assume that Salome and her sons hoped that Jesus would not refuse a mother's plea. To their dismay, Jesus could not grant them her request (Matt. 20:23). It becomes evident from the context that the disciple's view of success differed from Jesus' understanding. The disciples followed the ideals of secular rulers and officials (Matt. 20:25). They held the notion that whoever secured the place of prominence and authority would capture greatness.

Jesus took the opportunity to share His view of greatness with them. In His discourse the Lord establishes three fundamental ingredients needed to secure true greatness. They are servitude, submission, and surrender.

SERVITUDE

The mother's request meant relegating everyone else to a second-class position. Their undertaking had the potential of destroying any unity that had developed among the disciples. Obviously, it was essential that Jesus meet this problem head on. In a very real sense, the advice Christ was to share would make or break the future of Christianity.

If He had granted the request, surely jealousy, infighting, and maneuvering for power would have characterized the group. As so often was the case, the Lord proclaimed the unexpected by saying,

> *You know that the rulers of the Gentiles lord it over them, and their high officials exercise authority over them. Not so with you. Instead, whoever wants to become great among you must be your servant.* (Matt. 20:25-26)

If I had the opportunity to observe the reactions of the apostles, this would be one of those select occasions. The picture that comes to mind is one of James, John, and their mother staring in disbelief at the words of Christ. Rather than ascending to heavenly heights, they found themselves descending to greatness. Christ points out that the descent to greatness begins by becoming a servant.

A servant was someone who would voluntarily or involuntarily serve someone else.

While serving, their main interest was to promote and uphold the interests of someone else. Often a servant was required to perform the lowest of deeds (Luke 15:15), or experienced degrading abuse (20:11-12). The Lord illustrates the role of a servant when He said,

> *Suppose one of you had a servant plowing or looking after the sheep. Would he say to the servant when he comes in from the field, "Come along now and sit down to eat"? Would he not rather say, "Prepare my supper, get yourself ready and wait on me while I eat and drink; after that you may eat and drink"? Would he thank the servant because he did what he was told to do? So you also, when you have done everything you were told to do, should say, "We are unworthy servants; we have only done our duty."*
>
> (Luke 17:7-10)

This helps us better understand the path to greatness as seen through Christ's eyes. He teaches that, like a servant who has spent his day plowing or looking after the sheep, a disciple must be prepared to faithfully complete whatever task He has given us to do (v. 7).

Jesus then adds that once the servant has completed his task, he must be prepared to do even more (v. 8). A faithful servant is to focus on the needs and wants of his master. When all is said and done, the faithful servant should not expect even a thank you (v. 9-10).

In order to be great in His kingdom, we must be prepared for a life of humble servitude. If we are truly faithful in fulfilling our responsibilities, we should not expect special treatment for doing that which we are told.

SUBMISSION

The descent to greatness begins with servitude and continues with submission. Jesus says, *"whoever wants to be first must be your slave"* (Matt. 20:27). What is a slave? A slave is a person who has no claim on his life because he is literally the property of someone else. A slave does not receive a salary or vacation time. A slave is under bondage. If someone wants to express kindness to a slave, then the slave receives kindness. If, on the other hand, someone chooses to discipline a slave, then the slave is disciplined. A slave has no rights!

Joseph is a perfect example of this when he was falsely accused by Potiphar's wife. Time after time she insisted that Joseph sleep with her, but he refused to sin. Joseph fled, but she grabbed his cloak and presented it to her husband as proof that Joseph attempted to take advantage of her. Joseph was sent to prison without the opportunity to defend himself. Slaves have no rights or control over the affairs of their lives; they must continually stand in a position of submission.

Think about how James and John must have felt to hear Christ's directive. One moment they sought a position of great honor and authority, and the next they were told they must become servants and slaves. Surely James, John, and their mother felt humbled by the Lord.

SURRENDER

The Lord now turns from encouraging the apostles in the areas of servitude and submission to remind them of His life example. He makes it clear that *"the Son of Man did not come to be served, but to serve"* (Matt. 20:28). Jesus not only prescribed a life of humble servitude and submission, but was the very embodiment of it. Of course at that time no one realized just how much Christ had humbled Himself. None of the apostles had grasped the fullness of the Lord's condescension.

The Lord of glory left His heavenly throne to walk the earth in the humble form of a man. In doing so, Scripture says that Jesus was made *"like his brothers in every way"* (Heb. 2:17), and that *"because he himself suffered when he was tempted, he is able to help those who are being tempted"* (v. 18). When Christ walked this earth, He became as we are yet did not fall to sin. He understands our suffering and temptations. He tasted the curse of death. Therefore, we can never say to Him, "Jesus, you just don't know what it's like." He does know what it is like because He experienced a degradation we will never comprehend.

Consequently, when Jesus instructs us to pursue a life of humble servitude, He speaks not with empty words, but rather with the voice of experience. True greatness begins with servitude and submission but finds its culmination in complete surrender.

The surrender which our Lord spoke of is the relinquishing of our lives. Jesus went to the cross to die for our sins; in doing so, He illustrated the cost of true greatness. If we are to obtain the sort of greatness He offers, we must be willing to follow His example. True surrender means giving up everything, including your life, for the sake of serving others.

This is a foundational truth. We cannot descend to Christlike greatness if we are not prepared to embrace this truth.

As Americans, we do not normally associate words like *servitude*, *submission*, and *surrender* with words such as *success* and *greatness*. In this world such things are diametrically opposed to one another. Imagine engaging in such practices during a sporting event such as basketball. You have the ball, time is running out, and the score is tied. Whoever makes the next basket wins the National Championship. Instead of taking the final shot to win the game, you deliberately hand the ball over to the opposing team and wish them luck.

Undoubtedly the reaction of your teammates would be one of shock and outrage. Would their response be justified? Most certainly. When someone goes contrary to the purpose of the game, such a reaction must be expected. In basketball, as in all facets of life, the purpose is to win (become great) by outscoring (subduing) the other team. During Christ's stay here on earth, He redefined the rules of the game by commanding His followers to put aside the prominent social, cultural, and religious patterns they had grown accustomed to, in order to truly follow Him.

The Lord knew these instructions would spark opposition. Jesus warned us a time would come when

> *Brother will betray brother to death, and a father his child. Children will rebel against their parents and have them put to death. All men will hate you because of me, but he who stands firm to the end will be saved.* (Mark 13:12-13)

Everyone who plays by His rules ceases to play by the world's rules. If you cease to play by the rules of the world, you will be hated. The game plan is what separates the eternally successful from the eternal failures. The road to true greatness and success is found by following Christ's plan. If in your heart you are seeking to descend to Christlike greatness, you must endeavor with all your heart to serve as a servant, to submit as a slave, and to surrender your entire life, no matter what the cost.

SOURCES AND SIGNS

BEFORE SHE DIED IN THE CONCENTRATION CAMP MY SISTER BETSIE SAID TO ME, "CORRIE, YOUR WHOLE LIFE HAS BEEN TRAINING FOR THE WORK YOU ARE DOING HERE IN PRISON...AND FOR THE WORK YOU WILL DO AFTERWARD." THE LIFE OF A CHRISTIAN IS AN EDUCATION FOR HIGHER SERVICE.[9]

CORRIE TEN BOOM
WWII CONCENTRATION CAMP SURVIVOR
—IMPRISONED FOR HIDING JEWS

Many young children enjoy playing with stuffed animals because they are soft and cuddly. The cushy feeling is produced by the stuffing packed inside the animal. On several occasions I have watched an adventurous young child extract the stuffing from a toy animal. Bit by bit, with an air of persistence, the child pulled at the stuffing until there was nothing left. To his amazement, the little friend had become flatter than a pancake. Clearly, the child did not understand the importance of the stuffing. If he had, he would have left the contents where they belonged. By pulling out the stuffing, the composition of the toy was drastically altered.

Biblical success is much like a toy animal in that its sources and signs are the "stuffing." If we fail to recognize their importance, our understanding will be seriously altered.

During the days of the steam-powered trains, the rugged vehicles transported men, machines, and materials across the United States. The train's presence not only helped to shape the direction of our country, but also played an important role in settling the western frontier. Like all vehicles, the steam engines needed a source of power. The source most commonly used was coal. The coal would be used in fires meant to boil water which in turn created enough steam to cause a train to move. If biblical success were a steam-powered train, the sources of power would be the Cross, the Spirit, and the Word.

THE CROSS

The Cross of Christ is the place of our beginning. Without it there would be no salvation, no transformation, no hope. The Cross initiates the potential for success. Without it, eternal success is impossible. This powerful potential was initiated by defeating death and sin once and for all. It was accomplished by the Lamb of God through the sacrificial shedding of His blood, death upon the tree, and resurrection three days later. In Revelation 20:14 we see the culmination of this great victory described by the apostle John when he says, "*Then death and Hades were thrown into the lake of fire. The lake of fire is the second death.*" Death was absolutely conquered, and rendered harmless forevermore. Thankfully, there is no need to fear, for the impossible has been made possible because of the Cross.

THE SPIRIT

If the potential for success was initiated at the Cross, then it is stimulated through the ministry of the Holy Spirit. Like a giant fan, the Spirit of God takes the flame started at the Cross and blows it into a living fire. Jesus acknowledges this by stating that, "*The Spirit gives life; the flesh counts for nothing*" (John 6:63). Through the ministry of the Holy Spirit, those who are spiritually dead, those who are living in their sin, those who are without hope

111

find life. The Spirit opens the door of true success in them by means of the gracious gift of saving faith.

THE WORD

The Cross initiates, the Spirit stimulates, and the Word of God cultivates the potential for success. The Word works its way into the innermost part of man, seeking to solidify the success made evident in the life of a new believer. In 2 Timothy 3:16-17, Paul says,

> *All Scripture is God-breathed and is useful for teaching, rebuking, correcting and training in righteousness, so that the man of God may be thoroughly equipped for every good work.*

Here the apostle pictures the Word as the instrument of cultivation in the life of a believer. The purpose of the spiritual cultivation is to produce spiritual fruit, or in this case, "good works."

The Cross, the Spirit, and the Word make a very powerful threesome. The unity of their efforts can take the vilest person, bring him to salvation, transform his life, and establish his spiritual maturity. In the whole of the universe there is nothing more powerful or influential in the life of man. The Cross, the Spirit, and the Word are the source of eternal success. One cannot stand without the other; each has a vital role. We can be thankful to God for the presence of their ministry in a world void of true success.

A sign is a very important means of communication. Traffic signs help bring order to our streets and highways. Restaurant signs tell us what sort of food and service a particular place provides. The sign in front of a doctor's office helps us determine whether the doctor is a dentist or surgeon. They help us understand the physical health and well being of our bodies. There are certain signs which help doctors determine the condition of an individual. If a doctor can determine the symptoms, he can then make a prognosis.

It is important to remember that there are signs which help us distinguish those who are spiritually healthy from those who are not. If someone is growing spiritually, they will display at least three basic signs of growth: spiritual maturity, spiritual relationships, and spiritual gifts.

SPIRITUAL MATURITY

The condition of spiritual maturity is one that all true believers hunger and thirst for in their lives. Spiritual maturity is developed and advanced through a consistent and harmonious relationship with Jesus Christ. In short, the spiritually mature are those who have accepted Christ as Lord and Savior, learned what it takes to please Him, and are in process of doing so. Within the realm of spiritual maturity, there are many things which contribute to the growth of a believer. Of those things, there are several characteristics which stand above the rest.

PERCEPTION

Our perception of God and His view of reality dictates the type of relationship we will have with Him. If we misperceive who He is and what He stands for, our relationship with Him will be distorted. If we maintain a biblical understanding, the possibility of a healthy relationship is greatly enhanced.

Some believe God to be nothing more than the product of an overactive imagination. Others recognize His existence but do not believe we can have a personal relationship with Him. There are those who see Him as the God of the Bible but fail to recognize His authority. Our perception of reality determines the sort of relationship we will have with Him. The Lord has a perfect grasp on all aspects of reality.

Man, on the other hand, lacks the ability and vantage point to relate to His level. Yet in our frailty, we tend to act as if our insights are superior to His.

Peter's experience is a perfect example. One day shortly after Jesus had predicted His death, Peter challenged Jesus saying, "*Never, Lord!...This shall never happen to you!*" (Matt. 16:22). Realizing the error of Peter's statement, the Lord rebuked him:

> *Get behind me, Satan! You are a stumbling block to me; you do not have in mind the things of God, but the things of men.* (Matt. 16:23)

Why did Jesus refer to Peter as "Satan"? Peter wasn't Satan. He did so because the moment Peter spoke, Christ knew the apostles' perception of reality was distorted. Jesus realized that Peter was led by the flesh, not the Spirit. Jesus referred to Peter as Satan because he acted as an agent of Satan by attempting to deter God's will.

If we are not for God, we are against Him. If we do not encourage His will, we are discouraging it. There is no middle ground. We are either furthering the cause of Christ or that of His adversary the Devil. When Peter told the Lord that He would never go to the cross, he was toying with God's plan of salvation. Jesus fully grasped the big picture; Peter did not. The Lord knew that He must go to the cross if man was to be saved. At that point, Peter lacked the ability to comprehend this greater reality.

When viewing reality from man's limited perspective, the Lord's announcement indeed sounded foolish. Here Jesus was telling His disciples that He was going to suffer and be put to death. What sort of good news or encouragement was that? The disciples had given up everything to follow Jesus. The last thing they wanted to hear was the Lord talking about dying. He was supposed to be the Messiah spoken of in the Old Testament. They could not see any good coming from such a tragedy because they did not have eyes of faith.

The apostle Paul describes the perceptual platform all non-believers work from, saying,

> *They are darkened in their understanding and separated from the life of God because of the ignorance that is in them due to the hardening of their hearts.*
> (Eph. 4:18)

Man's view of reality is *darkened* or distorted because he views things through a heart and mind corrupted by sin (2 Cor. 5:16). Paul then informs us of the direction each of us must strive for by saying,

> *Put off your old self, which is being corrupted by its deceitful desires; to be made new in the attitude of your minds; and to put on the new self, created to be like God in true righteousness and holiness.*
> (Eph. 4:22-24)

The "old self" being "darkened" by sin cannot perceive reality properly because of self-deception. One aspect of the "new self" is a spiritual adjustment to "the attitude of your minds." This change of attitude constitutes a change in the way we perceive reality. The change is a result of the Holy Spirit causing the heart and mind to become sensitive to the Word of God (1 John 2:27).

As a result, we are no longer blind to God's reality but rather begin to see things through His eyes. Faith enables us to see things we never saw before and do things we never would have previously considered. The means to such change is based on our willingness to submit to Christ and follow Him. The

117

motivation to submit is intensified by the depth of our perception of God's reality.

In other words, the more we view life as God views it, the greater our desire becomes to align ourselves with Him and His Word. This takes place and develops as we faithfully request it through prayer. Therefore, if we lack godly zeal and growth, it is because we have failed to request them of God (James 4:2-3; 1 John 5:14-15).

PRIORITIES

As a person comes to Christ and begins to mature spiritually, not only his perception of reality changes, but his priorities do as well. Many of these changes occur immediately at the point of salvation, others later throughout the course of the believer's walk. When considering the importance of re-establishing our priorities, the Bible encourages us to do so in many areas.

The area that stands above the rest is following Christ. The phrase "following Christ" denotes the sort of relationship we may have with Him. A person who follows Christ maintains a high level of commitment to Him. In the literal sense of the word, a follower follows. Being a true follower may be easy or very difficult. For instance, if the person being followed makes his way to a swimming pool on a very hot day and jumps into the pool, following that person will be a very refreshing experience. On the other hand, if that same person makes his way to a swimming pool filled with piranhas, following that person will not be nearly as refreshing. A true follower follows, no matter what the cost.

When Jesus calls us to follow Him, if we agree to do so, by our actions and profession we are saying, "Lord, no matter what You do or where You go, no matter how easy or difficult, I will follow You, because following You is my primary purpose in life."

What sort of priorities does the Lord expect of a follower? He says to the rich young ruler, *"If you want to be perfect, go, sell your possessions and give to the poor, and you will have treasure in heaven"* (Matt. 19:21). He tells a potential disciple, *"Let the dead bury their own dead, but you go and proclaim the kingdom of God"* (Luke 9:60). He challenges the apostles saying, *"Now that I, your Lord and Teacher, have washed your feet, you also should wash one another's feet"* (John 13:14). When the Lord calls people to follow Him, He demands they reorder their lives and priorities. Jesus sums up things by saying, *"If anyone*

119

*would come after me, he must deny himself and
take up his cross and follow me"* (Matt. 16:24).

Christ speaks frankly when He challenges
us to follow Him. The Lord makes it clear that
the true follower is characterized by the priorities he or she maintains. Jesus tells us that
the true believer is willing to deny self in order
to pursue Him. Self-denial, Matthew Henry
once said, "is the fundamental law of admis-
sion into Christ's school, and the first and
great lesson to be learned in this school."[10]

The school he refers to is the school of
discipleship. Within this school, followers learn
the intricacies of following. The first lesson
learned is self-denial. The purpose of self-
denial is not starvation, poverty, or hermit-
like seclusion, but the re-ordering of our
earthly priorities.

The first and foremost of these priorities
is to serve and glorify our Master. How successful one is at accomplishing this priority
depends largely on the level of self-denial
exhibited.

The second lesson is taking up our cross.
Taking up the cross alludes to the Roman cus-
tom of the condemned carrying their crosses to
the place of execution. In doing so, the person
carrying the cross suffered the pain and hu-
miliation of bearing it, and worse yet, dying on

it. The symbolism of the cross directs us to the priorities of someone en route to their execution. He has only one purpose, and that is to die. The true disciple not only denies self but dies to self as well. The product of self-denial and taking up the cross is that we are prepared to follow in the footsteps of our Master. As He suffered, we must suffer. As He died, we must die. The first priority of a follower is to follow. The great tragedy of Christianity is that many people who claim to be Christians have never been followers.

You may uphold a form of Christianity, but if your number one priority in life is anything other than following Jesus Christ, you had better stop and re-examine your relationship with Him. If you have accepted Jesus as your Lord and Savior and bear proof of it (Matt. 12:33, 35) by daily serving and becoming more like Him, you may rest assured that you are a true follower.

If the majority of your life consists of pleasing self or someone other than Christ, you have not denied self. If the thought of submitting to Christ sickens you, you have not died to self. If you have never accepted Christ as Lord and Savior, you are not a follower. Through His death, the Lord has made it possible for each of us to become followers and re-establish our priorities. The Lord is calling. Have you heeded His call? Do your priorities reflect a true relationship with Him? Have you been a faithful follower?

PRAYER

A sure sign of spiritual maturity is a life permeated by prayer. Those who are, and have been, truly successful in God's eyes have understood the place and necessity of prayer. One such individual was a man named E. M. Bounds. Whether serving as a pastor, writer, or chaplain during the Civil War, prayer was at the forefront of his endeavors. Dr. Bounds is best remembered for his writing on the subject of prayer. In his book *"Power Through Prayer"* he characterized truly successful servants of God by saying,

> These men prayed not occasionally, not a little at regular or at odd times; but they so prayed that their prayers entered into and shaped their characters; they so prayed as to affect their own lives and the lives of others; they so prayed as to make the history of the church and influence the current of the times. They spent much time in prayer, not because they marked the shadow on the dial or the hands on the clock, but

because it was to them so momentous
and engaging a business that they could
scarcely give over.[11]

While portraying the prayer life of a successful servant, Dr. Bounds established four
important traits of the spiritually mature. He
begins by saying that they "prayed not occa-
sionally." Moses spent entire days and nights
before God in prayer (Exod. 24:18). Daniel met
with Him three times daily (Dan. 6:10). Even
Jesus would go to the mountain for long periods of time (Matt. 26:39-44). During a time of
tremendous distress, King David did not plot
ways to bring down his enemy but spent his
time praying. David points out the extent of
his prayer, "*I call to God, and the LORD saves
me. Evening, morning and noon I cry out in
distress, and he hears my voice*" (Psa. 55:16-
17). King David, the leader of a mighty army
could have sought deliverance by force, but
instead he opted to pray.

The spiritually sound are those who spend
a large amount of time in prayer. They do so
because they love to commune with God. The
ministry of prayer requires an abundance of
time. It is a labor which is never satisfied with
scanty efforts or half-heartedness. The will-

ingness to joyfully set aside time for prayer is
the mark of the truly faithful.

The spiritually mature are those whose
character has been shaped by prayer. They
have realized that the pathway to spiritual
growth is paved with prayer. Apart from
prayer, it is impossible to develop godly character. On the night of Jesus' betrayal, He demanded that Peter, James, and John sit at the
base of the mount to *"keep watch"* and *"pray"*
(Mark 14:34, 38) because He sought to influence the disciples' character.

Christ realized that genuine prayer was so
powerful that it could deliver them from temptation. Prayer shapes character in many ways.
The ministry of prayer teaches and strength-
ens our faith in God's ability to provide. It also
teaches us humility and dependence on Him.
All of this and much more work to develop and
strengthen a Christian's character.

Those who are spiritually mature have
come to realize that prayer not only carries
special benefits for them but for others as well.
Thus, the true man or woman of God seeks to
daily affect the lives of others. There are many
examples of intercessory prayer found
throughout Scripture. We see Samuel praying
on behalf of Israel when they demanded a king
(1 Sam. 8:6). King Hezekiah prayed that God

would spare Israel from the hands of Sennacherib (2 Kings 19:14-19). While being stoned to death, we see Stephen asking the Lord to forgive his murderers (Acts 7:60).

Time and again we see faithful men of God seeking to affect the lives of others through prayer. Scripture tells us, *"The prayer of a righteous man is powerful and effective"* (James 5:16), because the righteous man is spiritually mature. Those who are spiritually mature maintain an active prayer life and realize that failure to pray is based on selfish and misguided priorities.

If the righteous man is not praying, how is the power and effectiveness of his prayers to be unleashed? It won't be. Thus, those who are spiritually mature are compelled to pray because they realize the seriousness of neglecting such an important ministry. Having seen and tasted the benefits of prayer, it is difficult to see it as anything less than essential. For the spiritually mature, feasting in God's presence is a source of delight and nourishment.

One prayer warrior that comes to mind is David Brainerd. During the early days of our country, Brainerd, a missionary from New England, sought to minister to the Indians. Jonathan Edwards depicted Brainerd thus:

His life shows the right way to success in the works of the ministry. He sought it as the soldier seeks victory in a siege or battle, or as a man that runs a race for a great prize. Animated with love to Christ and souls, how did he labor? Always fervently. Not only in word and doctrine, in public and in private, but in prayers by day and night, wrestling with God in secret and travailing in birth with unutterable groans and agonies, until Christ was formed in the hearts of the people to whom he was sent. Like a true son of Jacob, he persevered in wrestling through all the darkness of the night, until the breaking of the day![12]

The intensity of Brainerd's prayer life was forged in his love for God. His love rendered him helpless apart from prayer. Prayer was much more than something tacked on at the beginning or end of the day. For David Brainerd, prayer was a matter of urgency and attraction.

On his death bed in 1688, John Bunyan, the English preacher and author of *Pilgrim's Progress*, recommended these timeless thoughts on prayer:

In all your prayers, forget not to thank the Lord for his mercies. When thou prayest, rather let thy heart be without words than thy words without heart. Prayer will make a man cease from sin, or sin will entice a man to cease from prayer. The spirit of prayer is more precious than thousands of gold and silver. Pray often, for prayer is a shield to the soul, a sacrifice to God, and a scourge for Satan.[13]

A God-pleasing prayer life is an important sign of spiritual maturity. As we seek to grow and develop in Christ, let us listen to and follow the example of those who have gone before us. Let us use prayer to influence the lives of our friends, family, and the world around us.

BIBLE STUDY

A corresponding sign of spiritual maturity is the desire to read God's Holy Word. Bible study is essential, because through it we receive God's Word. God uses the Bible to communicate those truths that help us grow and maintain a healthy relationship with Him. By combining Bible study with prayer, we establish two-way communication with God. The Lord speaks to us through Scripture, and prayer enables us to speak to Him. God has graciously provided a means of communicating with Him any hour of the day or night. All we have to do is read His Word or pray. Since the creation of Adam, our Father has longed for fellowship with His children.

Likewise, those who are spiritually mature view Scripture as a lamp before their feet and a light unto their path (Psa. 119:105). The lamp is capable of leading and guiding them through a journey filled with many pitfalls and snares. The "light" of the Bible helps them overcome the evil one who seeks to ensnare and devour believers. Those who have spiritually come of age approach the Word as a dry sponge, always thirsty and ready for more. When questions of God's will arise, they do not consult tea leaves and horoscopes. Instead, they confidently search His Word to find His perfect will.

The legendary preacher Charles Spurgeon once said,

> If you would know experimentally the preciousness of the promises, and enjoy them in your own heart, meditate much upon them. There are promises which are like grapes in the wine-press; if you will tread them the juice will flow.[14]

The Word of God makes no promises to those too lazy to study it. But for those willing to make reading a priority, *"it gives under-standing to the simple"* (Psa. 119:130). Who are the simple? Those who are uneducated in the Word. God promises that no matter how uneducated, if you study His Word, He will give you understanding. The Lord uses His Word in many ways. By it we learn of salvation (1 Pet. 1:23); it helps us grow (Acts 20:32; 1 Pet. 2:2); it brings prosperity (Josh. 1:7-8); and it helps us during times of sorrow (John 14:1), worry (Matt. 6:25-31), emptiness (John 15), and discouragement (Isa. 40).

APPLICATION

Mature Christians not only understand the importance of studying God's Word but of application as well. Reading Scripture without applying it is like a starving man reading a menu while refusing to order from it. Everything he needs to solve his dilemma is within his grasp. All he needs to do is act on it. Unfortunately, too many Christians approach Bible study just that way. Rather than studying and applying God's Word to their lives, they get close to the Word but do not allow it to change their lives. Scripture can do many things for us, but its healing balm is released only when we meditate on and apply it to our lives.

We see a note of frustration in Paul's words to the Corinthians when he says,

> *Brothers, I could not address you as spiritual but as worldly—mere infants in Christ. I gave you milk, not solid food, for you were not yet ready for it. Indeed, you are still not ready.*
>
> (1 Cor. 3:1-2)

The apostle is upset with the Corinthians because they have shown little diligence in the application of God's Word. Paul had hoped by this time they would have digested the "milk" and grown as a result. But to his dismay, they had not accomplished even that. The Word of God was not powerful and active in their lives, rather it was stale and inactive. In contrast, look at the spiritual maturity of the Bereans. Scripture says,

> *Now the Bereans were of more noble character than the Thessalonians, for they received the message with great eagerness and examined the Scriptures every day to see if what Paul said was true.*
>
> (Acts 17:11)

It is important to note that the Bereans received Paul's teaching *"with great eagerness."* They were filled with much anticipation and were glad to have the opportunity to hear his message. Likewise, upon hearing the Word, they compared the apostle's teaching with Scripture. They compared Scripture with Scripture in order to test the validity of Paul's message. Also, the Bereans were not satisfied with merely studying the Word but applied it as well. We know this to be certain because they *"were of more noble character."* The nobility spoken of here was a product of their desire to be in harmony with the Word of God. Thus, they not only studied the Word but applied it to their lives as well. As we consider the example of the Bereans, let us be found examining the Scriptures every day. Let us be known as people who love God and His Word so much that we not only study it, but allow it to promote growth in all areas of our lives.

CHEERFUL GIVERS

The spiritually mature are cheerful givers. Scripture tells us, *"Each man should give what he has decided in his heart to give, not reluctantly or under compulsion, for God loves a cheerful giver*" (2 Cor. 9:7). There is no need to twist arms or toy with guilt for the Spirit is alive and moving them to do that which pleases God. To man, a gift is a gift. But to God, who knows the heart, the validity of a gift depends on our inner motivation. If our giving lacks sincerity and graciousness, then in God's eyes our gift is worthless.

The greatest and most cheerful provider of gifts is God (1 Tim. 6:17). The Bible tells us, *"He causes his sun to rise on the evil and the good, and sends rain on the righteous and the unrighteous"* (Matt. 5:45). Since the early days of man, He has graciously provided for those who hate and despise Him. Even the most vile offender has benefited from His graciousness. The epitome of His graciousness was seen in the giving of His only Son to die on the cross. The Lord loves a cheerful giver because a cheerful giver is emulating Him. By imitating God, we glorify Him and provide an example for others to follow.

As we are consistent in our giving, we prove ourselves to be faithful stewards. A steward is someone who manages the affairs of another. From a Christian perspective, all believers are stewards of the gifts and blessings God has shared. The mature steward sees such things as belonging entirely to God, yet entrusted into his care. Because everything the steward possesses belongs to God, the faithful steward naturally renders to God that which is His.

Scripture says, *"Honor the LORD with your wealth, with the firstfruits of all your crops"* (Prov. 3:9). The standard for giving is seen in the rendering of our "first fruits" to God. When the faithful steward returns a portion back to God, he thinks in terms of offering the first and best of all he has. The Lord considers anything less than our first fruits to be an act of spiritual immorality. In the book of Malachi, the Lord condemns the priests for allowing the people to offer their leftovers. He says,

> *"When you bring injured, crippled or diseased animals and offer them as sacrifices, should I accept them from your hands?"* says the LORD. *"Cursed is the cheat who has an acceptable male in his flock and vows to give it, but then sacrifices a blemished animal to the LORD."*
>
> (Mal. 1:13-14)

Proper giving is so important to Him that at times He cursed those who cheated Him. We should never be fooled into believing that God cares little about our giving. The Lord cares a

great deal about our giving. When considering
the level of our giving, the Bible speaks of
tithing. The Word *tithe* indicates the setting
aside of or a tenth of our income. Tithing is
both practiced and commanded in Scripture.
Abraham gave Melchizedek the priest a tenth
of everything he owned (Gen. 14:20; Heb. 7:2).
Later God instituted tithing as a regular prac-
tice for the people of Israel (Deut. 14:22-29).

The early church also prescribed a tithe
for its members. Yet it differs from Old Testament regulations in that ten percent was
seen as an absolute minimum from one's total
income. In an early church document known
as the *Didache*, it "prescribed that first fruits
be given of money, clothes, and of all your possessions." Generally speaking, the tithe was
not meant to be a maximum level of giving,
but rather a minimum standard.

Thus, based on the teaching of Scripture
and church history, we may conclude that
tithing the first and best of our income is a valid
starting point for God's people. As we seek to offer God the best of our first fruits, there are several areas of giving we must account for.

Cheerful givers make **time** for God. They
are known to attend their local church functions
faithfully, maintain regular personal and family
devotions, and involve themselves in God's min-

istry. They are able to do so because their lives revolve around serving God. Bystanders might say they have no life outside the church, but in reality, they live as they do because they are sold on Christ and consider their life His. As a result, they order their lives around God and His work. To them there is no greater joy than serving the Lord and ministering to His people. They also realize that their ministry here on earth could end at any moment, and thus seek to make the most of the time allotted here.

Think of the saints who gathered to hear Paul speak at Troas. Scripture says,

> *On the first day of the week we came to-*
> *gether to break bread. Paul spoke to the*
> *people and, because he intended to leave*
> *the next day, kept on talking until mid-*
> *night...Then he went upstairs again and*
> *broke bread and ate. After talking until*
> *daylight, he left.* (Acts 20:7, 11)

As eventful as this meeting was, imagine Christians today having such a giving spirit that they would sit and listen to one man speak an entire night. If we attempted such a thing today, few would tolerate even Paul speaking for more than an hour, let alone an entire night. The believers of Troas exempli-

135

fied a willingness to freely give of their time. Their actions were based on a true love and hunger for God, His Word, and His messenger. Like those from Troas, men and women who love the Lord will prove it by faithfully setting aside time for Him.

One of the potentially most volatile issues within a church is the subject of **money**. While I served on the pastoral staff of one church, a survey was taken regarding the worship services. Several people had mentioned that the pastor spoke too much on the subject of stewardship. I couldn't help but marvel, for he had shared only three or four messages on the subject over the three years prior. For some people, one message a year is one too many! There are those who believe speaking on the subject of tithing is so taboo that it doesn't matter who is sharing the message, with what approach, or in what setting. More times then not, such people have not truly surrendered their finances to Christ. They fail to do so because deep down they believe their possessions actually belong to them.

Unlike their weaker brothers, those who are spiritually mature do not haggle over their resources because they have laid everything at the feet of Jesus. The cheerful giver gives a tenth of his money to support the ministry of the local church. He does so because he realizes that God's primary means of ministering to both Christians and non-Christians is through the local church. Often the cheerful giver is able to set aside additional money to help support other organizations such as Christian radio and television, missionaries, evangelists, and relief programs. The ministry of cheerful giving is a vital ministry. Much good has been done by the many faithful stewards of Christ.

Each of us is born with an aptitude for certain **talents** which are natural or acquired abilities. The cheerful giver cultivates his or her talents for the purpose of glorifying God through opportunities to minister to others. Some of the greatest blessings bestowed upon us are those cheerful givers who lend their talents. I have known of skilled tradesmen giving freely of their trade to help a Christian brother or sister in need. The church as a whole has been blessed countless times by those sharing their gifts in music.

Let us never forget the lesson of the parable of the talents (Matt. 25:14-30). The Lord wants each of us using what He has given us for His glory. It is a sin to bury our talents in the ground for safe keeping. Whatever the Lord has given, we must prosper for His glory.

Since He has given us talents, let us humbly use them as He provides opportunity!

Cheerful givers give praise to God through **body and mind** for the physical and mental health He has bestowed upon them. In a day when substance abuse is rampant, the spiritually mature avoid such foolishness. They do so because they realize their bodies are temples of the Holy Spirit (1 Cor. 3:16-17). God has provided us with our bodies, and it is our responsibility to care for them properly.

The Lord also wants us to care for and develop the minds He has graced us with. Some are born with greater intellectual capacities then others, but each of us needs to develop what we have been given for His glory. The greatest way we may give of our minds is to allow the Holy Spirit to renew and align our thoughts and knowledge in accordance with God's Word. The apostle Paul says,

Do not conform any longer to the pattern of this world, but be transformed by the renewing of your mind. Then you will be able to test and approve what God's will is—his good, pleasing and perfect will.
(Rom. 12:2)

The renewing of the mind is portrayed as an act of will. When a person becomes a

Christian, God does not treat him as a computer, commanding His Spirit to forcibly insert a new program into his "memory." The Spirit guides the believer while allowing him the choice of obeying or rejecting His leadership. The spiritually mature may not always experience smooth sailing, but through faith and obedience, they continue to be transformed by the renewing of their minds.

The Lord has blessed His people abundantly. He has provided us with an ever present example of giving. He has blessed us with the gifts of time and resources. The cheerful giver emulates God by faithfully returning to Him a portion of each of these gifts. The mature giver not only gives, but he always gives the first and the best of what he has.

The Lord calls each of us to be cheerful givers, continually maturing in our faith. Are you a cheerful giver? Do your possessions belong to you or God? Do you obediently give of your time, money, talents, body, and mind? The choice is yours to make.

FRUIT OF THE SPIRIT

Have you ever considered the difference between a diamond in the rough and one that has been skillfully cut? One is coarse, jagged, and contains many imperfections. While the other is beautifully smooth, distinct, and lacks imperfections. The main difference between the two is one has been skillfully fashioned by the hand of a master cutter, and the other has not. Thus, one is nearly worthless, while the other is of great worth. The Spirit's fruit (Gal. 5:22-23) is much like a well-cut diamond. Each characteristic is like a costly jewel. They are beautiful, distinct, and stand as a tribute to the Master Cutter. Upon becoming a Christian, the Master immediately begins to develop the fruit into the very essence of the believer. The presence of the fruit bears witness to the reality of the Master's presence in our lives. Just as it takes time to properly cut a diamond, it also takes time to carefully fashion fruit in the heart of a new believer. If the believer is resistant to the Master's efforts, progress will be slowed. To prevent that, we must seek to daily submit ourselves to the skillful touch of the Spirit as He shapes and forms us into the image of Christ.

The apostle Paul informs us that the Spirit's fruit is love, joy, peace, patience, kindness, goodness, faithfulness, gentleness, and self-control; all of which are key elements.

The first and most important characteristic is **love**. Love gains it prominence in that it links us to the very essence of God, for *"God is love"* (1 John 4:8). Love is a binding agent. It unites the saved to their Savior, the fellow to the fellowship, and the crusader to the cause. Love not only binds, but it separates as well. It distinguishes the saints from the sinners, the hopeful from the hopeless, and the sincere from the slanderer. True love is found only through a personal relationship with Jesus Christ. People may exhibit a form of love, but if it is not grounded in Christ it is a fleeting imitation. True love is affirmed not in sensuality, affections, or personal gain, but rather in submission and obedience to God.

Love for God may be expressed in many ways. Socially, we show Him love by loving other Christians, neighbors, and even our enemies. Spiritually, we demonstrate our love by studying His Word, praying, and sharing the gospel. Financially, we may offer love by faithfully supporting our local churches, Christian ministries, world missions, and the needy. As a church body, we may display love for the Lord by maintaining godly order, discipline, and growth.

As we seek to love the Lord, we must continually focus our actions on those around us.

All believers in Christ must aspire to be lovers of men. True love must be fostered and propagated in the local church for it should be the calling card of the church and those in it. Because God is the author of love, our concept of it must be seen through His Word. Thus, as we observe true love, we must acknowledge the threads of holiness, purity, and righteousness woven into its fabric. True love is opposed to evil (Psa. 97:10), upholds Scripture (Psa. 119:163), and never promotes ill will (Rom. 13:10). The love which God inspires encourages peace (Psa. 119:165), forgiveness (Prov. 10:12), mercy (Dan. 9:9), service (Gal. 5:13), fellowship (Phil. 2:1-2), and so on. The ultimate description of love is seen in the frequently cited passage in which Paul says,

> *Love is patient, love is kind. It does not envy, it does not boast, it is not proud. It is not rude, it is not self-seeking, it is not easily angered, it keeps no record of wrongs. Love does not delight in evil but rejoices with the truth. It always protects, always trusts, always hopes, always perseveres.* (1 Cor. 13:4-7)

Without a doubt, love is the foundation on which all else rests. It is love that draws and holds all else together. Without true love, there is no God, no salvation, no church, no ministry, and there is no hope! As inadequate as our love may be, as immature our understanding, if the fruit of the Spirit is to come alive in us, we must submit to love and allow it to lead us down the path of righteousness. As true love takes hold of our lives, spiritual maturity will take root in our hearts.

Joy transcends external giddiness and internal "warm fuzzies" because it is rooted in one's relationship with God. Therefore, it may be influenced by our circumstances and surroundings but is not determined by them. True joy rests in the assurance of salvation and finds comfort in God's sovereign rule. Because joy finds its basis and fulfillment in Jesus Christ, our hearts may delight in the victory we've obtained through Him even amid great trials and temptations.

The apostle Paul writes to the Corinthian church *"in all our troubles my joy knows no bounds"* (2 Cor. 7:4). Obviously Paul's life was filled with times of uncertainty, fear, and heartache. But even during such times, he relied on the *"God, who comforts the downcast"* (2 Cor. 7:6) to comfort him and encourage a gladness of heart. As true joy manifests itself in our lives, we cannot help but want to share the richness of its blessing with others. The joy of salvation and the comfort of Christian fellowship must inspire us to share a grace too wonderful to hoard.

The word **peace** indicates a form of contentment, wholeness, and harmony. It is a sense of friendliness and order between two or more parties. In order for us to gain true peace, we must first be in harmony with God. Scripture says that Christ *"is our peace"* (Eph. 2:14) because through Him we gain eternal life and are made complete. True peace is a product of His salvation. Once we are on "friendly" terms with Jesus, living a life of inward and outward peace becomes possible.

As we develop in our relationship with the Lord, through His Word and the empowering of His Spirit, we become more inclined to be at peace with those around us. The writer of Hebrews commands us to *"make every effort to live in peace with all men and to be holy"* (Heb. 12:14). The "effort" is emphasized over accomplishment, for the author knows it takes two agreeable parties to make peace. At times we may strive to keep peace, but others might not allow it. He also realizes that keeping peace is not always the godly thing to do. If keeping peace means disobeying God's Word, then peace becomes a secondary priority.

Therefore, our lives are to reflect Christlike peace while maintaining harmony with His Word.

Patience is possible only through a strong reliance on the Lord. The ability to wait on Him is based on an accurate understanding of His sovereignty. The degree to which we believe He is in control will at least partly determine our level of patience. In many places Scripture encourages us to be patient. Paul instructs the believers in Ephesis to *"be patient, bearing with one another in love"* (Eph. 4:2). To the Colossians he says, *"clothe yourselves with...patience"* (Col. 3:12). Patience is a characteristic which can help us weather many a rough and stormy sea.

The trait of personal **kindness** implies "goodness in action." Every time we are gracious, caring, and useful to those around us, we are expressing kindness. It may include signs of affection, but more importantly, it is seen through relevant and practical actions! As we seek to be kind to others, let us strive to flavor our deeds with the tenderness and compassion granted us by the Lord.

When used to express the Fruit of the Spirit, **goodness** is considered both a moral and a physical quality. The expression or attribute of goodness is noted especially in God.

When the Rich Ruler came to Jesus and said, *"Good teacher, what must I do to inherit eternal life?"* the Lord responded with, *"Why do you call me good? No one is good—except God alone"* (Luke 18:18-19). God alone is good, in the sense that He alone is absolutely good. God in His totality is good. By nature man is not good. Therefore, any goodness we express is the result of His grace.

It is essential to realize that good deeds in and of themselves do not automatically warrant God's approval. Why is this? Because the Lord knows our motives. If our motives for doing good works are anything less than glorifying God, then He does not honor our efforts. In order to glorify Him we must first be saved. Through salvation comes the potential to glorify God. Once saved, we must rely on the Holy Spirit to direct our motives. As we submit our will to Him, He is able to help us glorify God through the goodness wrought within our hearts. Why is goodness so important? Because Scripture says, *"For we are God's workmanship, created in Christ Jesus to do good works which God prepared in advance for us to do"* (Eph. 2:10). One of our primary purposes in life is to do good works. It is through such things God is lifted up, and we become people who love what is good (Titus 1:8).

Faithfulness is the quality of fidelity, which is made up of loyalty and trustworthiness. It indicates the degree of devotion to our duty and those we serve. The New Testament contains several examples of faithfulness. The apostle Paul refers to Timothy as one *"who is faithful in the Lord"* (1 Cor. 4:17); to Tychicus as a *"faithful servant in the Lord"* (Eph. 6:21); to Epaphras *"a faithful minister of Christ"* (Col. 1:7); and to Onesimus as *"our faithful and dear brother"* (Col. 4:9). Jesus expects an attitude of loyalty and trust to be at the center of our Christian experience.

The word **gentleness** denotes the idea of humility, meekness, and consideration. It is important that we do not associate such things with weakness or frailty. Jesus Christ was a "man's man." The Carpenter was rugged and capable of living under very difficult circumstances. Single-handedly, He stood up against some of the most prominent and influential leaders of His day. On two occasions, He cleansed the temple by overturning tables and forcing people out with a whip. The Lord was tough, yet gentle. He was firm when He had to be firm, yet maintained an inner meekness. Gentleness does not negate manliness, zealousness, or righteous anger. Instead, it seeks to temper and balance such traits.

Self-control is the concept of personal inward strength and temperance. It is the ability to exercise control over ones actions, attitudes, and thoughts. The ability to gain such control comes from the empowering of the Holy Spirit. The object of self-control is to maintain balance. At the heart of Christlike perfection, we see absolute balance. The Lord Himself was a picture of perfection, and this state of perfection is most readily seen in the balance Jesus daily preserved. Godly balance helped keep Jesus from losing control. And it is Christlike balance that can help us do the same.

The Lord through His Spirit encourages spiritual maturity in all true believers. As we grow and develop in righteousness, the fruit of the Spirit becomes more and more evident throughout all areas of our lives. As we seek to grow and develop in Christ, let us beseech the Spirit to help us put on love, joy, peace, patience, kindness, goodness, faithfulness, gentleness, and self-control.

Each of us enters Christianity like a diamond in the rough. We are not smooth and polished but spiritually rough and jagged. Like the uncut diamond, it does not matter how many years we have been a diamond, what matters most is what the Master Cutter has been able to do with us during those years.

The Lord has found some of us easy to cut and fashion into His likeness, while others have been much more difficult. Rather than resisting God, let us endeavor to be jewels which are easy to work with—objects of great worth with His fruit engraved into the depths of our souls.

SPIRITUAL RELATIONSHIPS

One of the clearest signs of true success is the development of spiritual relationships. When someone becomes a Christian, the desire to establish spiritual relationships is almost instinctive.

"Fellowship" maintains a host of meanings and may be applied in many ways. The Greek word most commonly used to express the concept of fellowship is *koinonia*. It conveys a sense of association, community, communion, and joint participation. A similar word, *koinonos*, carries with it the idea of being a partaker, partner, companion, or comrade. The bedrock of Christian fellowship is a living and active relationship with the Father. The apostle John says, *"our fellowship is with the Father and with his Son, Jesus Christ"* (1 John 1:3).

Salvation unlocks the door to fellowship in the church. Without it, we cannot partake of the blessings that accompany it. A person might be a church member, tithe regularly, teach Sunday School, and attend activities faithfully, but if he is not truly saved, he cannot enter into true Christian fellowship. The apostle John points out, *"If we claim to have fellowship with him yet walk in the darkness, we lie and do not live by the truth"* (1 John 1:6). In order to partake in Christian fellowship, we must be children of God, but in addition, we must be in harmony with Him. John goes on to say, *"But if we walk in the light, as he is in the light, we have fellowship with one another"* (1 John 1:7). The apostle promises that as we maintain consistency with the light, we will have fellowship with one another. What is the light he refers to? The light is God and His Word. In order to "walk in the light," we must be in harmony with the Bible. If we fail to do so, John says we are not in the light, but in darkness.

If we refuse to submit to God and His Word, our fellowship with others will be affected. Why? Because God will use their example to convict us of our sin, which then creates tension and discomfort within. The people God uses might not even know they are being used in this manner, but we will. We will be bothered by their consistency and higher standard and may even blame or resent them. But, in reality it is the Spirit using others to minister to our hearts. We must also walk in the light because this is the basis by which we conduct our fellowship. The Lord provides us with His Word, His Spirit, and His leadership to promote love, order, and harmony between those of like faith. He does so that we may experience true fellowship with Him and our brothers and sisters in Christ.

As we seek to engage in Christian fellowship, it is essential that we understand its composition. People often equate fellowshipping with socializing. It is true that socializing may be an element of fellowship, but Christian fellowship goes beyond merely socializing with other believers. The more our hearts and minds are harmoniously focused upon the Lord and His Word, the purer our fellowship will be, and the more it will maintain depth and meaning. At the heart of Christian fellowship is the goal of glorifying God. If our actions and attitudes do not conform to God's Word, then our fellowship is not Christlike. The Bible says, *"whether you eat or drink or whatever you do, do it all for the glory of God"* (1 Cor. 10:31).

Fellowship may take place in public or private settings because surroundings are not as important as the focal point of our energies. As we draw closer together and collectively focus our hearts and minds upon the Lord, we may be assured that our fellowship is sweet and savory to Him. A beautiful picture is seen in Acts:

> *They devoted themselves to the apostles' teaching and to the fellowship, to the breaking of bread and to prayer. Everyone was filled with awe, and many wonders and miraculous signs were done by the apostles. All the believers were together and had everything in common. Selling their possessions and goods, they gave to anyone as he had need. Every day they continued to meet together in the temple courts. They broke bread in their homes and ate together with glad and sincere hearts, praising God and enjoying the favor of all the people. And the Lord added to their number daily those who were being saved.*
>
> (Acts 2:42-47)

An exuberance, an excitement, a love, and a harmony typified this early gathering. They engaged in a fellowship that few today experience or understand. They were nourished spiritually by the teaching of the apostles, and physically by a common loaf. "Praising God" for His bountiful gift of salvation was the core of their fellowship. The level of fellowship which the early church experienced should not be seen as an exact model for churches today, but the principles of love, order, and general harmony should be sought after vigorously. As we draw closer to such ideals we too will know the joy of true fellowship.

At the heart of the Christian walk is the need to minister to others. The Lord made this clear when He announced the Great Commission.

> *Therefore go and make disciples of all nations, baptizing them in the name of the Father and of the Son and of the Holy Spirit, and teaching them to obey everything I have commanded.*
> (Matt. 28:19-20)

Some would believe that this commandment was directed only toward those who were to become full-time missionaries, but in actuality, it was a command for every person who knows Christ as Lord and Savior. The Great Commission is usually associated with sending missionaries to far away lands. Indeed, this is a noble and godly endeavor, but all true believers must realize their responsibilities in the ministry of personal evangelism. The apostle Paul gives perspective to this ministry when he says,

> *How, then, can they call on the one they have not believed in? And how can they believe in the one of whom they have not heard? And how can they hear without someone preaching to them? And how can they preach unless they are sent? As it is written, "How beautiful are the feet of those who bring good news!"*
>
> (Rom. 10:14-15)

Scripture requires the church to send missionaries not only throughout the world, but next door as well. Those waiting to hear the gospel need faithful servants of Christ to carry out the mission Christ has given them, that God's will may come to fruition. When we do so, we must not be *"ashamed of the gospel"* (Rom. 1:16) God has given us. For the gospel is the means by which *"God demonstrates his own love for us"* (Rom. 5:8). And as we obey His command, we demonstrate our love for Him and those around us. The result of our effort is answered in, *"How beautiful are the feet of those who bring good news!"* (Rom. 10:15). As we are faithful in our walk and our witness, we become a beautiful sight to all those who receive our message.

As men and women enter into Christ's kingdom, He demands that we raise them to grow and develop into mature disciples. The Lord said we must teach them *"to obey everything I have commanded"* (Matt. 28:20). The Lord's commission sets our priorities: new believers are commanded to learn, and those who have learned must teach.

The teaching He refers to does not necessarily demand a formal setting, but it does demand holiness, obedience, knowledge, and the will to minister. Why are such things so important? Because our model is what the new believer will learn from. Raising up new believers is much like training a new team member. When the player joins the team, he tends to model himself after players already on the team. If the older players maintain high standards, the new player strives to meet them. On the other hand, if the team has low standards, the new player is unlikely to go far beyond. This holds true for the church as well. If our example and standards are not up to par, those who follow our example will tend to follow suit. When churches wonder why certain problems and bad habits pass from generation to generation, it is often due to the example and pattern shared with new believers as they grow up or come into the church. The only way to break this cycle is for the church and its people to commit themselves to providing a pattern that reflects a Christlike example.

SPIRITUAL GIFTS

In his letter to the Ephesians, Paul helps us understand the importance of every Christian establishing themselves as ministers of Christ. He writes,

It was He who gave some to be apostles, some to be prophets, some to be evangelists, and some to be pastors and teachers, to prepare God's people for works of service, so that the body of Christ may be built up. (Eph. 4:11-12)

We see that God gave the church various types of leaders for the purpose of preparing His people for "*works of service.*" The Lord uses Sunday school classes, morning and evening services, and prayer meetings to equip His children to become effective ministers.

One way in which the Lord equips people to minister to one another is through the use of spiritual gifts. A spiritual gift is something freely bestowed upon a believer for the purpose of ministering to or on behalf of the church with the ultimate purpose of glorifying God. He gives these gifts through the Holy Spirit who is residing in the believer. Paul says of the gifts,

> *We have different gifts, according to the grace given us. If a man's gift is prophesying, let him use it in proportion to his faith. If it is serving, let him serve; if it is teaching, let him teach; if it is encouraging, let him encourage; if it is contributing to the needs of others, let him give generously; if it is leadership, let him govern diligently; if it is showing mercy, let him do it cheerfully.* (Rom. 12:6-8)

It is important to note that all true believers are given spiritual gifts (1 Cor. 12:11). We are all commanded to use them for the purpose of building up the body of Christ. The best way to determine our gifts is by growing in the Word and making ourselves available for service in the local church. As you do so, the Lord, and those in

leadership, will help guide in the acknowledgment of such things.

8

SNAGS TO SUCCESS

...LET US THROW OFF EVERYTHING THAT HIN-
DERS AND THE SIN THAT SO EASILY ENTAN-
GLES... LET US FIX OUR EYES ON JESUS...

HEBREWS 12:1-2

For those who enjoy the sport of fishing, there is no greater excitement then catching the "big one." As with most things in life, fishing has its setbacks. The most frequently encountered delay is snagging a line or hook on something. There are many objects to get snagged on—trees, underwater logs or rocks, other people, the boat or dock, and even the fisherman himself. Just as an experienced fisherman may encounter various obstacles, so too may the believer in Christ. Let's take a look at some of the most common snags.

SIN

The first and most common snag is sin. Adam and Eve were snagged by sin and therefore banished from the garden. Sin has subsequently ensnared the greatest of believers down through the ages. Moses disobeyed God by striking the rock (Num. 20:11), King David committed adultery with Bathsheba (2 Sam. 11:4), and Peter denied Christ (Luke 22:56-60). Each of these honored men were entangled by sin, and each paid dearly as a result. Like the fisherman, no one looks to be snagged by sin. It comes to us in many ways. Sometimes we lose sight of our God-ordained objective because of apathy or carelessness. Other times through outright foolishness. Sin is the root of all failure and being snagged is an ever-present danger in the life of a believer.

COMPETING INTERESTS

One of the most subtle snags to success is competing interests. It is incredibly easy for us to lose sight of our primary objective. Work, friends, recreation, hobbies, entertainment, and the like can rob us of the precious time needed to pursue our godly calling. In and of themselves, such things are not sinful. They become snares only when we allow them to dominate our lives. The fact is, too much emphasis on anything other than God deters us from success.

The key is balance, and Jesus was a man of perfect balance. The Lord prayed, read the Word, maintained fellowship, shared the gospel, healed the sick, and did many other valuable things. Jesus could very easily have spent every waking hour healing the sick. Think of the happiness and satisfaction in healing person after person, town after town. As noble and fulfilling as it would have been, Jesus did not spend the majority of His time healing. The Son loved spending time with His Father. Often, He would commit entire nights to prayer. The Lord could have given His life solely over to prayer and teaching, but He did not. Rather, with perfect balance, He prioritized and divided His time among His many competing interests. Why? Because He realized the necessity of a balanced life. Jesus said, *"The Sabbath was made for man, not man for the Sabbath"* (Mark 2:27).

Nothing, be it the Sabbath or anything else, was made to rule over man; such things were made to help him grasp eternal success. By His own example Christ encourages us to be men and women of balance. Let us make sure we do not become ensnared by our numerous interests, priorities, or concerns. Failure to do so will drive us from Christlike balance.

CULTURE

One of the most difficult snares to detect and overcome is the snag of culture. I am referring to the societal grid which makes up our system of beliefs, expectations, and norms. It tends to be passed from one generation to the next, and influences each person's life from birth to death. Many fail to see culture as a threat because it becomes so imbedded in our personalities that we are blinded to how it dictates our lives. At times we stand guilty of forcing our culture onto our faith.

While serving as a missionary in Africa, I had an opportunity to see the sort of influence culture can have on Christians. Early during my stay, I was informed by several nationals that it was wrong for men to wear shorts, because only boys wear short pants. Does the Bible teach that wearing short pants is sinful? Certainly not. Culture has raised the social rule to a moral standard.

As Christians, we must be very careful not to be swayed by such things. Rather, we must sift our entire belief system through the Word of God. Cultures come and go, and people change, but Scripture cannot be broken, because its principles are timeless.

SUCCESS

The last snag we will consider is success itself. As we have already noted, there are two forms of success: man's and God's. Each of us is very capable of pursuing worldly success. It is tempting and luring. Satan attempted to sway Christ when, *"the devil took him to a very high mountain and showed him all the kingdoms of the world and their splendor"* (Matt. 4:8). After doing so, the Devil said to Jesus, *"All this I will give you...if you will bow down and worship me"* (Matt. 4:9). Satan realized the grip worldly success could potentially have on men. Of course he was not dealing with just any man. He was dealing with the Son of God; thus his attempt to seduce Jesus failed miserably.

As certain as Christ's success was, man's is just that uncertain. We are overcome so easily. Even the "best" of us struggle. We see a clear example of this in the life of the apostle Paul. Shortly after Paul was *"caught up to Paradise"* (2 Cor. 12:4), God felt it necessary to afflict him with a thorn in the flesh. After being raised to the heights of glory, why was Paul afflicted with a thorn? Paul says, *"To keep me from becoming conceited"* (2 Cor. 12:7). But why? Because, like most of us, he struggled with the snag of success. Paul had been granted something few in history have experienced. Left to himself, the great apostle Paul would probably have become prideful.

If Paul could become ensnared by spiritual success, where does that leave us? How much more must we keep watch over ourselves. If the devoted Paul needed a single thorn, perhaps we might do well with four or five! Sad to say, any amount of worldly or spiritual success can become intoxicating. As a result, the more success God grants us, the more we must humble ourselves before His throne. There's an old saying, "Absolute power corrupts absolutely." In this case, success can be likened to power. The greater the worldly success, the greater the potential of spiritual corruption. Sin is at the heart of all failure, but as we have seen, competing interests, culture, and even success may derail us as well. Therefore, let us run confidently in Christ, being careful to avoid the many snags that Satan throws in our paths.

9

STANDARDS OF SUCCESS

I WILL DEAL WITH THEM ACCORDING TO THEIR
CONDUCT, ...THEN THEY WILL KNOW THAT I AM
THE LORD.

EZEKIEL 7:27

In all areas of life there are guidelines which govern the way we approach things. Within society there are governing authorities which the Bible encourages us to submit to (Rom. 13:1). Within Christianity, the Lord has established certain standards which, if followed, will help promote success in the life of the believer and the local church.

PUBLIC ACCOUNTABILITY

The first standard of success is public accountability. All people need to answer to someone other than themselves, in order to prevent their perspectives from becoming skewed. As Christians, we are commanded to submit to the accountability of others.

To Christ

First and foremost we are accountable to the Lord Jesus Christ. Our relationship and accountability to Him establishes the basis for all other relationships. The level to which we realize our accountability to Him, will tend to affect the way we respond to other areas of accountability. Consequently, the zeal or indifference we direct toward the Lord, will most likely find its way into other areas of our lives. The parable of the ten minas (Luke 19:11-26) makes it undeniably evident that He holds His disciples to a standard of accountability. The parable speaks of a nobleman traveling to a distant country in order to be appointed king. Prior to his departure, he summoned ten of his servants and gave them ten minas. He then commanded them to put the money to work until he returned. Upon his return, he summoned his servants to account for their use of his money. Jesus' point was to draw attention to His standard of accountability: *"to everyone who has, more will be given but as for the one who has nothing, even what he has will be taken away"* (v. 26).

The words of Jesus are very sobering. He makes it clear that we are accountable to use all that He has given us to glorify Him and further His interests. If we prove ourselves faithful in small things here on earth, He promises to bless us upon His return. On the other hand, if we prove ourselves unfaithful, we will suffer loss. The apostle Paul mentions this time of accounting by saying,

> *For we must all appear before the judgment seat of Christ, that each one may receive what is due him for the things done while in the body, whether good or bad.* (2 Cor. 5:10)

Each of us stands accountable first and foremost to Christ. Thus, let us make certain our priorities are in order. We have only one life to live and one opportunity to prove our faithfulness to our Master.

TO LEADERS

The Lord places men in positions of spiritual leadership to maintain biblical order and discipline within the church. The Bible establishes accountability between the believer and the leader by saying,

> *Obey your leaders and submit to their*
> *authority. They keep watch over you as*
> *men who must give an account. Obey*
> *them so that their work will be a joy, not*
> *a burden, for that would be of no advan-*
> *tage to you.*   (Heb. 13:17)

This statement clearly points out that
every believer is accountable to those charged
with their oversight. When we obey and submit to those in authority, we are doing it as
unto God. Just as civil authorities *"that exist*
have been established by God" (Rom. 13:1), so
too are spiritual leaders. The Lord commands
all believers to obey and submit, for apart from
such cooperation, godly order and discipline
within the church are impossible.

OTHER BELIEVERS

The Word of God not only establishes accountability between Christ, church leaders,
and the believer, but it also commands believers to account to one another. The Bible says,
"Submit to one another out of reverence for
Christ" (Eph. 5:21). As reverence for Christ is
the basis of our submission, the criteria which
governs it is the Word of God. Thus, for this to
become a reality, it is essential that we are in

agreement with the Word of God. The act of submission is something which is done voluntarily in the spirit of love, humility, and holiness. It is not contrived but generated from a heart of servitude. Its goal is the welfare and betterment of other believers. Therefore, Paul instructs with these words,

> *Do nothing out of selfish ambition or vain conceit, but in humility consider others better than yourselves. Each of you should look not only to your own interests, but also to the interests of others.*
> (Phil. 2:3-4)

True love, humility, and holiness encourage an atmosphere conducive to accountability, whereas selfish ambition and vain conceit rob us of the possibility.

PERSONAL ACCOUNTABILITY

The second standard of success is personal accountability. This involves the process of self-examination. As we enter into a time of personal examination, the Holy Spirit is free to probe our hearts and prompt our memories. The Spirit reminds us of our sins and encourages us to do something about them. We see a call to self-examination in 1 Corinthians. Where Paul speaks of the believers' need to check themselves prior to partaking of the Lord's Supper: *"A man ought to examine himself before he eats of the bread and drinks of the cup"* (1 Cor. 11:28).

Far too often believers are only encouraged to examine themselves before Communion. In reality, if we want to maintain a healthy walk with Christ, we must examine ourselves daily. In doing so, we guard ourselves from becoming callous to and accumulating undealt-with sin. Failure to deal with sin on a daily basis is the root cause for many of the problems we encounter, for sin tends to breed sin. One of the healthiest spiritual exercises is daily evaluation of the spiritual condition of our hearts, minds, speeches, senses, and actions. Sin that is confessed and repented of helps break this terrible cycle.

The Psalms are evidence that David believed self-examination was important. At one point he requested God's guidance in helping him to examine himself. David petitioned God saying,

Search me, O God, and know my heart;
test me and know my anxious thoughts.
See if there is any offensive way in me,

and lead me in the way everlasting.
                    (Psa. 139:23-24)

May this likewise be our hearts cry! May we daily search our hearts for sinful motives and feelings, our minds for thoughts which are not pure, our lips for words which are not pleasing, our eyes and ears for the ungodly things we may choose to look at and listen to, and actions that may promote a bad example for others. Let us sweep out the old filth and garbage, and replace it with God's Word and the empowering of the Holy Spirit. In doing so we make it much harder for sin to find a nesting place within us. Do not forget Paul's exhortation, *"But if we judged ourselves, we would not come under judgment"* (1 Cor. 11:31).

PERSEVERANCE

The third standard of success is perseverance. In terms of Christianity, perseverance denotes the consistent and continual walk of faith which is both inwardly and outwardly expressed through the life of a believer. The perseverance of a believer is a product of genuine faith. The Lord points this out by saying, *"but he who stands firm to the end will be saved"* (Matt. 24:13), and *"If you hold to my teaching, you are really my disciples"* (John 8:31). The endurance of a believer and his commitment to Christ's teaching is the equivalent of saying "I am truly saved!" Signs such as these reinforce the validity of our claim to Christianity.

Whether we persevere through the *"light and momentary troubles"* that Paul speaks of (2 Cor. 4:17), or find our very lives taken away, the rewards of eternal glory far outweigh the trials, temptations, hurts, and pains we may experience here on earth. All those of true faith are encouraged, like Timothy, to

> *Endure hardship with us like a good soldier of Christ Jesus. No one serving as a soldier gets involved in civilian affairs—he wants to please his commanding officer.* (2 Tim. 2:3-4)

Each of us must come to the point where we reckon with the questions: "Am I enduring hardship like a good soldier?" "Are the affairs of my commanding officer, the Lord Jesus Christ, my number one priority?" If you are enduring to the end and fully embracing the Lord's teaching, then carry on, good soldier. But if not, your commanding officer wants to speak to you immediately. As you seek to serve Christ daily, remember that you are accountable to Him, to your spiritual leaders, and to other believers. Continually examine your heart, mind, speech, senses, and actions. Soldier, where do you stand amid the daily battles of life? Are you standing firm, or are you ready to turn and retreat? Take hope, Christian soldier, for the Commanding Officer stands beside you prepared to lead you on to victory!

10

WAGES AND REWARDS

BLESSED ARE YOU WHEN PEOPLE INSULT YOU,
PERSECUTE YOU AND FALSELY SAY ALL KINDS
OF EVIL AGAINST YOU BECAUSE OF ME. REJOICE
AND BE GLAD, BECAUSE GREAT IS YOUR
REWARD IN HEAVEN...

MATTHEW 5:11-12

When seeking to discern the means of obtaining success, there is a path which claims to guide us in the proper direction. The Bible says of this avenue, *"wide is the gate and broad is the road that leads to destruction, and many enter through it"* (Matt. 7:13). The wide gate easily ensnares the majority of people. It lures people through money, fame, power, sex, false religion, and so on. It uses greed, lust, deception, and manipulation to encourage us to pursue a success without success. This sort of success is as a dry oasis amid the desert of life. By obtaining such a prize, we may claim victory, but the horror of the conquest is only a heart beat away!

The Lord, in His graciousness, informs us that there is another option. He says, *"small is the gate and narrow the road that leads to life, and only a few find it"* (Matt. 7:14). The gateway He speaks of is the one that leads to eternal life. The only way to find it is to humbly follow the Good Shepherd, Jesus Christ. He alone is capable of leading us to and through the "narrow gate."

Part of following the Shepherd entails surrendering ourselves to Him, making Him Lord and Savior of our lives. As we seek to follow, the Shepherd warns us of the trials and tribulations that may await us.

Through His death on the cross, Jesus paid the price for man's sin. As a result, there is nothing we can do to earn our salvation. Jesus did it all. Yet this assurance does not nullify the fact that faithful disciples of Christ are expected to bear the **costs of true success**. The price we pay as disciples may take many forms, but we will limit our discussion to three aspects.

PERSECUTION

As we grow in faith and understanding, we begin to realize the importance of our public witness. The more we share the gospel with others, and the more we align ourselves with the truths of God, the greater the potential to become the object of persecution. Several years ago a friend of mine shared an incident that involved his brother who was a small-town pastor. His brother was a strong and forceful preacher. Because he preached with conviction, his messages did not sit well with everyone in town. This eventually led to a degree of persecution. On one occasion, the sheriff followed the preacher into a men's room and told him that if he did not pack his bags and leave town, he would make certain his name was ruined. Because the preacher did not heed the warning, the sheriff began to circulate a terrible lie about him. The pastor was not beaten or killed physically, but the sheriff did attempt to murder his reputation. When we faithfully preach, teach, or share God's Word, persecution may come.

For the most part it will take the form of verbal attacks, but we must always be prepared for much worse. While speaking to Timothy, the apostle Paul said,

In fact, everyone who wants to live a godly life in Christ Jesus will be persecuted, while evil men and impostors will

> *go from bad to worse, deceiving and be-*
> *ing deceived.* (2 Tim. 3:12-13)

Persecution frequently accompanies a godly lifestyle; often the more godly the life, the more the persecution. Paul says persecution will come from godless men. Those Paul speaks of will be living in the "last days." He says such people are

> *Lovers of themselves, lovers of money,*
> *boastful, proud, abusive, disobedient to*
> *their parents, ungrateful, unholy, with-*
> *out love, unforgiving, slanderous, with-*
> *out self-control, brutal, not lovers of the*
> *good, treacherous, rash, conceited, lovers*
> *of pleasure rather than lovers of God—*
> *having a form of godliness but denying*
> *its power.* (2 Tim. 3:2-5)

Interestingly enough, amid the many sins such people commit, Paul says they have "*a form of godliness*." This tells us that some of them appear to be "religious" people. In fact, some may be found in local churches. This may seem strange, but it was "religious" men who were responsible for the murder of Jesus. Consequently, those who truly pursue godliness may be persecuted not only from those outside the local church, but possibly from within as well.

How must we respond to such people? The apostle says, *"Have nothing to do with them"* (2 Tim. 3:5). Notice he does not encourage us to fight, argue, or seek revenge but simply, *"Have nothing to do with them."* And why must we heed such instruction? Because *"Bad company corrupts good character"* (1 Cor. 15:33). Paul is not interested in causing division, but if the church has made honest attempts to correct the wayward and if godly counsel is ignored, the church must seek to preserve its integrity and purity above all else.

LOSS

The apostle Paul tells us we must be prepared to suffer persecution. Along with persecution, we must be prepared to suffer loss. He says,

> *I consider everything a loss compared to the surpassing greatness of knowing Christ Jesus my Lord, for whose sake I have lost all things.*   (Phil. 3:8)

Paul spoke with the voice of experience. Religiously, he lost his pharisaic lifestyle and the many benefits that accompanied it. Culturally, he became a man without a country because the Jews considered his conversion as a denial of his heritage. Physically, he points out the loss of his creature comforts.

> *Five times I received from the Jews the forty lashes minus one. Three times I was beaten with rods, once I was stoned, three times I was shipwrecked, I spent a night and a day in the open sea, I have been constantly on the move. I have been in danger from rivers, in danger from bandits, in danger from my own countrymen, in danger from Gentiles; in danger in the city, in danger in the country, in danger at sea; and in danger from false brothers. I have labored and toiled and have often gone without sleep; I have known hunger and thirst and have often gone without food; I have been cold and naked.* (2 Cor. 11: 24-27)

Like Paul, our pathways to godly success may be paved with loss. For some it may mean the loss of family, wealth, possessions, or popularity; for others it may mean much more.

DEATH

Every believer in Christ experiences death. Scripture says,

> *For we know that our old self was crucified with him so that the body of sin might be done away with, that we should no longer be slaves to sin— because anyone who has died has been freed from sin.* (Rom. 6:6-7)

The death spoken of here is the death of carnal passions that go contrary to the ways of God. In order to enter God's family, by faith we must sacrifice the old self so that, through the power of the Holy Spirit we would no longer be slaves to sin but free to serve God. Believers must not only sacrifice the "old self" but be prepared to sacrifice the "new self" as well. Many times throughout history, true believers have been called on to surrender their lives. In *Foxe's Book Of Martyrs*[15] there are numerous accounts of Christians laying down their lives for the sake of the gospel.

The book of Revelation shows a glimpse of the many who were martyred because of their faith. There the apostle John says,

> *I saw under the altar the souls of those
> who had been slain because of the word
> of God and the testimony they had main-
> tained. They called out in a loud voice,
> "How long, Sovereign Lord, holy and
> true, until you judge the inhabitants of
> the earth and avenge our blood?" Then
> each of them was given a white robe, and
> they were told to wait a little longer, un-
> til the number of their fellow servants
> and brothers who were to be killed as
> they had been was completed.*
>
> (Rev. 6:9-11)

The "number" John spoke of continues to enter the ranks of martyrdom. A present-day example is seen in an article entitled "Freedoms
under Fire" by Timothy K. Jones. Mr. Jones
wrote of a pastor in the country of Peru being
tortured and killed by a terrorist group. The
reason for the murder was that young people
were coming to Christ through the pastor's
ministry. He noted that as a whole, "over 400
evangelicals have been killed by the group because of their faith."[16] Christians dying for
their faith is a modern-day reality!

Perhaps the Lord might call on us to enter
the sacred ranks the apostle John spoke of.
Jesus once said, *"Greater love has no one than
this, that he lay down his life for his friends"*

(John 15:13). Jesus is every Christian's friend. He proved His loyalty by dying in our place. If called upon, do you love your Friend enough to die for Him? Persecution, loss, and death are part of the cost of God-centered success. It is only a matter of time before such things enter the lives of all believers. Have you counted the cost of pursuing true success?

*****

The **rewards** of God-centered success are many. The depth and reality go far beyond mortal comprehension. God's blessings are not placed before us as enticement but rather to inform us of the Lord's great and glorious provision.

SONS AND DAUGHTERS OF GOD

The first and greatest blessing is the eternal satisfaction of sonship and daughterhood. *"I will be a Father to you, and you will be my sons and daughters, says the Lord Almighty"* (2 Cor. 6:18). John says of God's gift, *"How great is the love the Father has lavished on us, that we should be called children of God!"* (1 John 3:1). Most certainly, the love and the blessing of the Father are magnificent. To think He would allow such humble creatures to become sons and daughters forever! This truly is the gift of gifts. The blessing we shall receive is far greater than that of the poorest of children being adopted by the richest man. The King of Kings has chosen to take for Himself the most vile offenders, bathe them in the blood of Christ, clothe them in eternal garments, and place the mark of sonship upon them. Plainly, the significance of this gift is too great for mere words.

GOD'S PRAISE

The Word of God says that upon the Lord's return, He *"will expose the motives of men's hearts. At that time each will receive his praise from God"* (1 Cor. 4:5). Once judgment has been made, the most wonderful words any servant of Christ could hope to hear are, *"Well done, good and faithful servant! You have been faithful with a few things...Come and share your master's happiness!"* (Matt. 25:23). Knowing the praise of God awaits those who are truly faithful servants is more than enough to carry a believer through a life of trials and tribulation.

ETERNAL REST

The days of our lives are marked by pain, sweat, and toil. This is a direct result of Adam's sin. The Lord said to Adam, *"By the sweat of your brow you will eat your food until you return to the ground"* (Gen. 3:19). For the moment we may toil, but this is not the way it will always be. Scripture says, *"Blessed are the dead who die in the LORD...they will rest from their labor, for their deeds will follow them"* (Rev. 14:13). This rest will last an eternity. No longer will we engage in painful labor, barely able to make ends meet. Rather, one day we will enter into that perfect rest the Lord has prepared for us. The Lord said, *"In my Father's house are many rooms; if it were not so, I would have told you. I am going there to prepare a place for you"* (John 14:2). Happily He has promised to prepare a haven of rest for His disciples.

GLORIFICATION

The believer in Christ, as a child of God, receives His praise, enters His eternal rest, and one day shall be glorified by Him. The Bible says, *"those he predestined, he also called;*

those he called, he also justified; those he justified, he also glorified" (Rom. 8:30). The glorification we will experience centers around the redemption of our earthly body (Rom. 8:23). Paul says, *"For the perishable must clothe itself with the imperishable, and the mortal with immortality"* (1 Cor. 15:53). This glorified body will be perfect. It will never see sickness, decay, or even death. We will be made glorious and beautiful beyond human comprehension. One day we will be *"raised in power"* and clothed with a heavenly body (1 Cor. 15:43, 51-54). What a glorious and wonderful day that will be!

11

THE MASTER'S PATTERN

WAKE UP! STRENGTHEN WHAT REMAINS AND IS
ABOUT TO DIE, FOR I HAVE NOT FOUND YOUR
DEEDS COMPLETE IN THE SIGHT OF MY GOD. RE-
MEMBER, THEREFORE, WHAT YOU HAVE RE-
CEIVED AND HEARD; OBEY IT, AND REPENT. BUT
IF YOU DO NOT WAKE UP, I WILL COME LIKE A
THIEF, AND YOU WILL NOT KNOW AT WHAT TIME I
WILL COME TO YOU. HE WHO OVERCOMES
WILL...BE DRESSED IN WHITE. I WILL NEVER BLOT
OUT HIS NAME FROM THE BOOK OF LIFE, BUT
WILL ACKNOWLEDGE HIS NAME BEFORE MY FA-
THER AND HIS ANGELS. HE WHO HAS AN EAR,
LET HIM HEAR WHAT THE SPIRIT SAYS...

REVELATION 3:2-3, 5-6

For those who are true disciples of Christ, eternal success is an ongoing reality. It was secured for us roughly two thousand years ago on Calvary. The degree to which we enter into a life of success depends on the faithfulness of our walk with Him. As we identify and align ourselves with His priorities through godly obedience and submission, we will experience a life of true success. Obtaining success is not some sort of nebulous endeavor. Fortunately, God has provided a clear pattern we can follow.

FOCUS

The first step in God's pattern is to set our sights on Christ. We must actively choose to focus upon Him as opposed to peripheral concerns and interests. This involves an active and ongoing spiritual relationship with Him. For those who have accepted Christ, keeping our eyes on Him is a daily endeavor. There are many things in life that seek to draw our attention away from Him. We must resist turning away from Christ through prayerful submission to the Holy Spirit.

PRIORITY

The second phase to God's pattern for successful living is to establish godly order to our priorities. The first and most important priority we must uphold is living for Jesus. We must take time to fellowship daily with Christ, maintain our focus on Him, and make His concerns our concerns. If not, we fail to embrace the most basic elements of God's pattern for successful living. Regardless of the priority, Christ must always stand supreme. Likewise, when seeking to reorder our priorities, the Lord and His Word must determine the relevance and govern their makeup. If we allow factors beyond the Lord and His Word to shape us, our priorities will become skewed. In a world full of confusion and competing interests, only Christ can bring true order and harmony to the affairs and priorities of our lives.

BALANCE

Man by nature is prone to imbalance. When he experiences some sort of embarrassment, loss, or failure, rather than striving to obtain balance, often he embraces just the opposite. A very important element in God's pattern for successful living is godly balance. We are commanded to be perfect as Christ was. What is perfection? It is nothing more than absolute Christlike balance! Above all else, Jesus was a man who maintained absolute balance throughout His life. Unlike others, Jesus wasn't an extremist. The great sin of the Pharisees was imbalance. They were unsuccessful because they added to God's law. On the other hand, the Gentiles failed because they took away from God's perfect balance by ignoring God and His Word. True balance can only be found in the person of Christ. To succeed in this life, we must study and emulate His example.

MOTIVATION

At the heart of God's pattern for successful living is our motivation. Proper focus, priorities, and balance cannot be achieved apart from a God-centered motivation. The level of actual success we attain is determined by the essence of our motivation. Even as believers we can do the right things for the wrong reasons. If our pursuits are motivated by anything other than the desire to glorify God, we have failed in our endeavors. God gauges our success through the grid of exalting Him.

This labor of love must be waged on a moment-by-moment basis. Far too often we are apt to approach our walk from a daily perspective. But in reality, we must think in terms of seconds rather than days. With minds quicker than computers, our thoughts operate in split seconds, and our motivation can fluctuate just as quickly.

When praying, how often has your mind strayed from God? When reading the Bible, how many times have you entertained thoughts other than His Word? When listening to a message, how often have you daydreamed? All of us have succumbed to such momentary failures. We fail because our heart's motivation is quick to stray if unchecked. Consequently, we may physically take part in long periods of prayer, while spiritually failing to commune with God. We may read God's Word but fail to longingly meditate on it. We may warm the pew but not the heart. How is this possible? Through a lack of godly motivation bathed in love and a desire to glorify the Lord! Attempting to daily walk with God is a noble enterprise. To grasp success we must commit ourselves to achieving the small, momentary, and unseen victories of life. Obtaining true success demands a life of total dedication to Christ. God, in His graciousness, has not called us without establishing His means of provision. He has given the believer many tools to help achieve true success. As a result, we no longer have to settle for a success without success. We may claim His victory moment by moment, day by day!

Let us never settle for a success which is passing away but surrender to the love and grace which made true success possible. Together let us live the victorious life we have in Christ and share the abundance of that success with those around us. Our purpose is not to gain merit before God, but to glorify Him with all of our heart, soul, mind, and strength. Through us, may Jesus Christ be praised!

12

KEYS TO ETERNAL SUCCESS

I AM THE WAY AND THE TRUTH AND THE LIFE. NO
ONE COMES TO THE FATHER EXCEPT THROUGH
ME.

JOHN 14:6

Acquiring eternal success is much like gaining passage into a beautiful kingdom, a kingdom made accessible only by passing through a mighty door. The door, being the only entrance into the kingdom, is firmly secured. Because the kingdom is ruled by a very gracious king, the keys are accessible to all who request them. Like the gracious king, the Lord provides five important keys that open the door to eternal success. As we briefly look at each of the keys, remember, if you have never accepted Jesus as your Lord and Savior, you may do so simply by using the keys provided by God.

THE PROBLEM

The first key to eternal success identifies the problem that keeps us from attaining it. The Bible says, *"for all have sinned and fall short of the glory of God"* (Rom. 3:23). Everyone, without exception, has fallen short of matching and maintaining God's perfect standard of holiness, and it is His standard that all men shall be judged by. Heaven is God's dwelling place; because of His holy nature, only those who meet His standards are able to enter. The dilemma is that man is incapable of fulfilling God's standards. Recognition and acceptance of our sin problem is absolutely necessary to take the first step toward eternal success. Have you acknowledged before God that you are a sinner?

THE PUNISHMENT

The Bible says, *"For the wages of sin is death"* (Rom. 6:23). Every time we sin, we "earn" the wage of a sinner. The wage of a sinner is spiritual death and eternal separation from God. The place of punishment is the lake of fire, a place of continual suffering for all eternity. Man is sent there, not because God has wronged man, but because man has wronged God! Is such a strong punishment fair? Most certainly. As the most moral and just Being, God is more than capable of accurately determining and then punishing man's sin. He has concluded that because of our sin, each of us rightly deserves physical and spiritual death. Have you come to the place in your life where you can acknowledge that you deserve to be punished for your sin?

THE PROVISION

Provision enables us to overcome sin and punishment, thus granting eternal success. For centuries man longed to fly. Try as he might, he could not. Until the airplane was invented, flight was impossible. The airplane provided man with the ability to fly. Similarly, many have longed to enter the heavenly realm, but apart from God's transportation system, heaven is unenterable. Roughly two thousand years ago, God graciously sent His Son Jesus Christ to the cross. He allowed His Son to bear man's punishment that the free gift of eternal life might be extended to all. The Bible says, *"But God demonstrates his own love for us in this: While we were still sinners, Christ died for us"* (Rom. 5:8). Scripture also says, *"For it is by grace you have been saved, through faith— and this not from yourselves, it is the gift of God"* (Eph. 2:8).

The Lord did for us what we could not do for ourselves. The perfect God-Man paid the ultimate price for our sins by shedding His blood on the cross. Thus, He offered His life on our behalf. As a result, through our provision Christ, the kingdom of God and eternal success are now attainable.

THE PROMISE

God made a covenant with man. There is nothing mystical about claiming God's promise. Scripture says, *"For God so loved the world that he gave his one and only Son, that whoever believes in him shall not perish but have eternal life"* (John 3:16). The basis of God's promise centers around truly believing that Christ died to pay for our sins and that He overcame death through His bodily resurrection. Do you want to claim Christ's victory? You may do so by; (1) Recognizing and confessing your sinfulness to God, (2) Asking His forgiveness and cleansing, (3) Fully embracing

Christ's resurrection which defeated death and sin, and (4) Humbly turning from sin's rule in order to submit to Christ's loving oversight.

Acknowledge that apart from Him, eternal life and true success are impossible. Go to the Lord in prayer, and claim His free gift of salvation. Don't wait—do it now!

THE PURPOSE

The last key we must grasp is the purpose of eternal success. The Lord did not send His Son simply for us to claim success, but to live successfully. There are three basic elements to living a successful life in Christ.

The first element is sharing Christ with others. The Bible says, *"confess with your mouth the Lord Jesus"* (Rom. 10:9 NKJV). By sharing Christ with others, we proclaim our allegiance to Him. We enable others to know Him as well.

The second element is becoming like Christ in all areas of our life. Scripture says, *"Everyone who has this hope in him purifies himself, just as he is pure"* (1 John 3:3). The validity of our success in Christ is witnessed through a change in our heart's motivation and outward actions. Through obedience and submission to God and

197

His Word we prove the sincerity of our claim to be His followers.

The last and most important element is glorifying God. The essence of true success is found in seeking always to glorify God through our lives. Jesus said, *"glorify your Father in heaven"* (Matt. 5:16 NKJV). Scripture adds, "So *whether you eat or drink or whatever you do, do it all for the glory of God"* (1 Cor. 10:31). Man's first and most important priority in life is to exalt God in all things. The Lord has proven Himself to be a gracious and loving God. Countless times each of us have sought our own good while ignoring His. Rather than exalting Him, most spend their lives exalting themselves. Instead of seeking to further His interests, we get caught up in our own.

The Lord longs for a relationship with you. He has done everything possible to create one. Respond by embracing Him as your Lord and Savior. I urge you to go to Him this very moment in prayer in order to take hold of the success He has provided for you. In doing so, true success will forevermore be yours!

ENDNOTES

CHAPTER ONE
[1]Tim LaHaye, *Faith of Our Founding Fathers* (Brentwood, TN: Wolgemuth & Hyatt, 1987), 112.

[2]Walt Whitman, *Whitman: Poetry and Prose* (New York: Literary Classics of the United States, 1982), 188.

[3]Ibid, 244.

CHAPTER TWO
[4]Walter B. Knight, *Knight's Up-to-the-Minute Illustrations* (Chicago: Moody Press, 1974), 222.

CHAPTER FOUR
[5]John Gadsby, *Memoirs of the Principal Hymn Writers and Compilers of the 17th, 18th, and 19th Centuries* (London: John Gadsby, 1882), 53.

[6]*Bartlett's Familiar Quotations,* (Microsoft Bookshelf, 1993).

CHAPTER FIVE
[7]Jonathan Edwards, ed., *The Life and Diary of David Brainerd* (Grand Rapids: Baker, 1989), 180.

[8]Thomas O. Chisolm, *His Praise Anew* (Anderson, IN: The Gospel Trumpet, 1936), 75.

CHAPTER SEVEN
[9]Pamela Rosewell, *The Five Silent Years of Corrie Ten Boom,* (Grand Rapids: Zondervan, 1986), 77.

[10]Matthew Henry, *Matthew Henry's Commentary on the Whole Bible, Vol. 5,* (McLain, VA: MacDonald, 1706), 237.

[11]E. M. Bounds, *The Complete Works of E. M. Bounds on Prayer,* (Grand Rapids: Baker, 1990), 459.

[12]Ibid., 101.

[13]John Bunyan, *The Riches of John Bunyan* (Grand Rapids: Baker, 1978), 271.

[14]C. H. Spurgeon, *Morning and Evening,* (Nashville: Nelson, 1994), July 27, morning.

CHAPTER TEN
[15]John Foxe, *Foxe's Book of Martyrs* (Springdale, PA: Whitaker, 1981).

[16]Timothy K. Jones, "Freedoms under Fire," *Christianity Today* (July 20, 1992): 37.